TRAVELLERS

CHILE

By
NICHOLAS GILL

Written by Nicholas Gill

Original photography by Nicholas Gill

Editing and page layout by Cambridge Publishing Management Ltd,
Unit 2, Burr Elm Court, Caldecote CB23 7NU
Series Editor: Karen Beaulah

Published by Thomas Cook Publishing
A division of Thomas Cook Tour Operations Ltd
Company Registration No. 1450464 England

PO Box 227, The Thomas Cook Business Park,
Coningsby Road, Peterborough PE3 8SB, United Kingdom
E-mail: books@thomascook.com
www.thomascookpublishing.com
Tel: +44 (0)1733 416477

ISBN: 978-1-84157-819-4

Project Editor: Linda Bass
Production/DTP Editor: Steven Collins

Although every care has been taken in compiling this publication, and the
contents are believed to be correct at the time of printing, Thomas Cook Tour
Operations Ltd cannot accept any responsibility for errors or omissions,
however caused, or for changes in details given in the guidebook, or for the
consequences of any reliance on the information provided.

The opinions and assessments expressed in this book do not necessarily
represent those of Thomas Cook Tour Operations Ltd.

Printed and bound in Italy by: Printer Trento.

Front cover credits, L–R: © Fridmar Damm/Zefa/Corbis; © Wes Walker/
Lonely Planet Images/Getty Images; © Cozzi Guido/4Corners Images
Back cover credits, L–R: © Tony Waltham/Robert Harding/Getty Images;
© Gavin Hellier/Robert Harding/Getty Images

Contents

Introduction

Chile is a country unlike any other, with a windswept and wild terrain matched by a clash of cultures from European to indigenous. It's full of natural wonders and some of the world's premier resort areas. It's a country where poets dream and Catholicism mingles with folklore in a unique and magnificent spectacle.

Chileans are one of the most diverse groups of people in Latin America and numerous groups have come together over the past few centuries. Various indigenous groups lived in the north of the country and were eventually conquered by the Incas in the 15th century. The Mapuche, who defended their territory from both the Incas and the Spanish, controlled the southern half of the country until about 150 years ago. The Spanish influence is strong in many cities, although Chile's Criollo culture developed quite differently from that of neighbouring Peru, which was Spain's South American capital during the conquest.

Santiago is one of the most exciting capitals in Latin America. The city is bringing South American culinary achievements to a new level, with some of the best restaurants in the world. Here you will find everything from world-class museums to 5-star hotels aimed at business travellers. Except for a few major port areas, much of the rest of the country is rural and dotted with holiday resorts, spas and lakeside retreats. Nature is intertwined with luxury at an extreme level. There is no better place than Chile to get away from it all, as many celebrities, presidents and diplomats have already discovered.

The country is one of the most protected in the world and national parks are everywhere. Torres del Paine in the extreme south and Parque Nacional Lauca in the extreme north are two of the best examples, and offer scenery quite different from each other. Wildlife is abundant here: camelids such as vicuña and guanaco roam freely in the north and the south of the country. The Andean condor, threatened in many parts of the continent, thrives in Torres del Paine and other protected areas. Penguin colonies dot Patagonia and the entire coast.

The country holds some of the best hiking, rafting, kayaking, climbing, paragliding, fishing and skiing in the world. Olympic ski teams make Chile their off-season base, and several speed records have been broken here. The Río Futaleufú is a mecca for whitewater rafters, while the hiking infrastructure in Parque Nacional Torres del Paine allows you to hike for ten hours in a day and stay the night in relative comfort with hot showers and gourmet meals.

The country is isolated by oceans, mountains, deserts and ice. However, cosy buses make travel a breeze, while planes and ferries cut around the ice in the south so you can set foot in the world's final frontier. The strong, modern economy has kept the country from the crime and poverty that has stricken the rest of Latin America and added a tourist infrastructure on a par with the Western world. Although only averaging 180km (112 miles) wide at its biggest point, this is a country filled with nature such as volcanoes, glaciers, fiords, forests, lakes and wildlife reserves. You can paraglide off of a sand dune or kayak with penguins. It is a nation like nowhere else on earth.

Introduction

Norte Grande, Parque Nacional Lauca, Volcán Parinacota and Volcán Pomerape

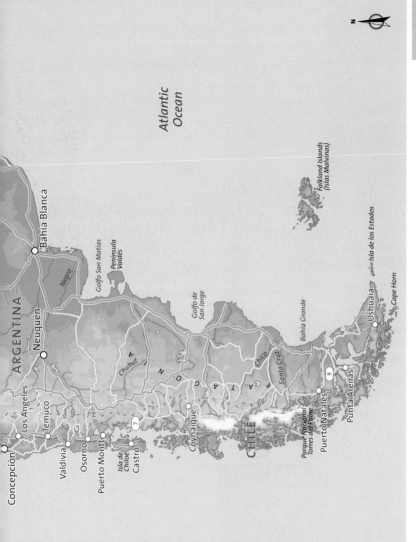

Atlantic
Ocean

Falkland Islands
(Islas Malvinas)

ARGENTINA

Bahía Blanca

Neuquén

Los Angeles

Temuco

Valdivia

Osorno

Puerto Montt

Isla de
Chiloé

Castro

Coyhaique

CHILE

Parque Nacional
Torres del Paine

Puerto Natales

Punta Arenas

Ushuaia

Isla de los Estados

Cape Horn

Concepción

Negro

Golfo San Matías

Península
Valdés

Golfo de
San Jorge

Bahía Grande

Chubut

Chico

Santa Cruz

P A T A G O N I A

0   250km
0   125 miles

The land

Wherever you are in Chile, you are near at least one great natural location. The north is filled with deserts and fertile valleys, while the south is green and forested, culminating on rocky fiords and azure blue glaciers. The geography has shaped the lives of Chile's people, as earthquakes and volcanic eruptions have displaced towns and cities, whilst shaping the countryside to form one of the world's most exotic settings.

Climate

The coastal north enjoys a cool, rain-free climate for much of the year, with only a rise in temperature during the summer months. Slightly inland in the Altiplano (high plain), there are distinct rainy (December–March) and dry seasons (May–October). Central Chile, south of La Serena, enjoys a Mediterranean-like climate with rainy springs (November–December), warm and at times blazing hot summers (January–February), crisp and cool autumns (March–May) and mild winters (June–October). In Patagonia you can see all four seasons in a day, with the chance of snow at higher altitudes existing year-round. The summer temperatures rarely rise above 15°C (59°F) and daylight extends to nearly midnight.

Most say the best time to visit Chile is in the summer months, when the whole of Patagonia opens up. However, many prefer the winter, when the ski resorts are in full swing and national parks such as Torres del Paine lack the large crowds and high prices of the summer.

Geology

More than 40 glacial periods have shaped Chile over the past seven million years, particularly in the south, where remnants of the last period, approximately 15,000 years ago, have been found. The Andes Mountains are relatively young in the scope of geology, rising just 35 million years ago as the South American plate began to rise over the Nazca and Antarctic plates.

Glacier Serrano in Parque Nacional Bernardo O'Higgins

Atacama Desert scenery near San Pedro de Atacama

Volcanoes cover the landscape from north to south, many pluming with smoke, and have led to geysers and natural hot springs. Earthquakes are not uncommon and the strongest earthquake ever recorded, 9.5 on the Richter scale, occurred here on 22 May 1960.

Landscapes

Stretching more than 4,270km (2,650 miles) from the near tropics to the Antarctic, Chile has one of the most diverse landscapes in the world. Its narrow width means that you are never very far from the Pacific in the west or the spine of the Andes in the east.

In the north of the country, along the Peruvian and Bolivian borders, the Altiplano is a high-altitude, barren land of volcanoes and lakes, which attracts a unique blend of wildlife. From here, the Andes run along the eastern side of the country, on the border with Argentina and, at times, venture to the coast. Many of the mountains rise above 6,000m (19,685ft), such as the country's highest peak, Ojos del Salado

(6,880m/22,572ft), and are covered in snow and crowned with glaciers. Along the northern coast the Atacama Desert, considered to be the driest place on earth, covers most of the landscape. The desert isn't empty, though: there are strange rock formations, sand dunes, boiling geysers, the largest salt flats in the country and highly valuable nitrate and copper deposits.

The fertile central valleys are home to the majority of the population and are the agricultural heart of the country. Green pastures and superb farmland sit beside temperate forests and highland lakes. The capital is here, as well as the world-renowned vineyards that stretch side by side for kilometres. The Lakes District combines stunning mountain scenery dotted with picture-perfect lakes that have made it the premier holiday destination for many Chileans and adventure seekers.

The mysterious island of Chiloé hangs off of Puerto Montt. Often covered in mist and rain, the island is covered in hills and a pathwork of farms that sit along charming bays. In the south, much of Patagonia is filled with impassable mountain ranges and ice fields. It is a place of extreme diversity as glaciers and lush temperate forests can all be found throughout the region and long stretches of flat farmland fill the extreme south. Patagonia isn't the end of the line. Chile ends at the South pole, and the nation is one of the many that have claimed a piece of Antarctica.

History

15,000–10,000 BC	First humans make their way to Chile from the north.

10,000–5,000 BC	Paleo-Indian culture develops in the Norte Chico, as mega fauna such as the Milodón and American Horse begin to die out.

5,000 BC–AD 500	Chinchorro culture in Northern Chile. People develop mummification process. El Molle culture develops ceramics.

AD 500–1450	Small civilisations begin to appear across the country. The Aymara in the north, the Atacameños and Diaguitas further south, the Mapuche south of Santiago to Patagonia, and the ice fields by the Yámana, Selk'nam, and various small groups.

1450–1500	The Incas invade northern Chile, but are stopped from pushing further south by Mapuche Resistance.

1520	Ferdinand Magellan passes through the Straits of Magellan, becoming the first European to see Patagonia.

1536	Spaniard Diego de Almagro arrives overland from Peru, passing over the Andes during harsh winter weather to the valley of Copiapó, exploring parts of Central Chile, before returning north through the coastal desert.

1540–42	Pedro de Valdivia sets out from Peru and founds Santiago de Chile on 12 February 1541, before being burnt down by the Mapuche soon after. It was quickly rebuilt as a fort and the native populations were subdued.

1552	Spanish settlements expand south with the founding of Valdivia. Mapuche Cacique Lautaro, after six years of imprisonment by the Spanish, escapes and teaches his people military strategy, including riding horses.

1553	Mapuche uprising under Lautaro and Valdivia is killed.

1567 Chiloé Island is claimed by Spain and becomes the southernmost European settlement.

1578 Francis Drake attacks the coasts of Chile, La Serena and other cities are plundered.

1598–1608 Mapuche uprisings drive the Spanish north of the Río Biobío for the next two and a half centuries.

1722 Rapa Nui (Easter Island) is discovered by Dutch navigator Jacob Roggeveen on 5 April.

1767 The Spanish empire exiles all Jesuits.

1810–18 The Criollos (people of Spanish ancestry, but not born in Spain) of Santiago proclaim a governing Junta. The battles of Maipú and Chacabuco assure independence and on 12 February 1818, Bernardo O'Higgins signs the Declaration of Independence.

1820–24 Independence movements across South America expel Spain from the continent.

1834–35 Charles Darwin and the HMS *Beagle* sail along the coast.

1844 Spain recognises Chilean independence.

1879–84 Chile defeats Peru and Bolivia in The War of the Pacific, adding nearly a third to its territory. Nitrate mines are soon discovered which drive the economy forward until the present day.

1904 Pablo Neruda is born in Parral, in Southern Chile on 12 July.

1904–1906 Labour unrest. Soldiers fire on meat workers and saltpetre workers in what has become known as the Meat Massacre in Santiago and Massacre of Escuela Santa María in Iquique.

1945 Gabriela Mistral receives the Nobel Prize for Literature.

1946 Gabriel González Videla becomes president. He caves in to pressure from the US and puts into effect the Law of Defence of Democracy, outlawing his former Communist and Radical allies, some of whom are being placed in concentration camps in Pisagua. Pablo Neruda goes into exile.

1960 The Great Chilean Earthquake near Valdivia, is the strongest ever recorded, measuring 9.5 on the Richter scale.

1970 Salvador Allende of the Unidad Popular elected president, becoming the world's first democratically elected Socialist leader.

1971 Pablo Neruda receives Nobel Prize for Literature.

1973 Army General Augusto Pinochet leads the bloody

Palacio de la Moneda, the site of the 1973 coup lead by General Pinochet

US-supported coup d'etat on 11 September, raiding the presidential offices as Allende commits suicide.

1973–89 Pinochet's 17-year reign is steeped in terror. Thousands are tortured and killed, Congress is dissolved and leftist parties are banned.

1978 Near war with Argentina over the Beagle Channel.

1989–97 Pinochet is ousted by Christian Democrat Patricio Aylwin, in the country's first free elections in two decades. Pinochet maintains control of the army and elects himself Senator in 1997.

1998 During a visit to London for medical reasons, Augusto Pinochet is arrested on the orders of a Spanish judge investigating the disappearance of Spanish citizens during the 1973 coup. US President Clinton releases files depicting 30 years of US involvement and covert aid to undermine Allende.

1999 Pinochet returns to Chile and all charges are dropped, as he is declared unfit to stand trial because of his deteriorated mental state. He steps down from his Senate seat due to his condition. Chile suffers greatly from the world economic crisis, resulting in years of inflation and unemployment.

2003 Chile signs a free trade agreement with the US.

2004 More than 28,000 former political prisoners during Pinochet's rule are granted financial compensation by Congress. A divorce law is granted for the first time in the country's history.

2004–2007 The Chilean Supreme Court declares that Pinochet is mentally competent to stand trial, but he dies on 10 December 2006, before ever going to court. Celebrations ignite in the streets across the country. In 2006, Michelle Bachelet, a former political prisoner under Pinochet and a single mother of three, becomes Chile's first female president.

Politics

The coup on 11 September 1973 that ousted Socialist President Salvador Allende became a dictatorship that dissolved Congress and spun a tangled web that is only now beginning to unweave. During that time politics was put on the backburner as power abuses were common and fear and torture took root.

From 1979 to 1989, the right-wing military government moved away from statism towards a free market economy that saw an increase in both domestic and foreign private investment, while the copper and nitrate industry remained nationalised. With Pinochet's fall from power and the return to democracy in 1989, the Republic has moved back to the left and military power has gradually faded.

In 2005, President Ricardo Lagos signed several constitutional amendments that included eliminating the positions of appointed senators, the presidential authority to remove heads of the armed forces, and reducing the presidential term from six to four years. Current President, Michelle Bachelet, was elected in January 2006 after receiving 53.49 per cent of the vote. Her term will continue until 2010. She is the fourth president from the Concertación coalition, which is made up of the Christian Democratic Party (PDC), the Party for Democracy (PPD), the Socialist Party (PS) and the Radical Social Democratic Party (PRSD).

Everything is not perfect, however. Indigenous groups such as the Mapuche are being ignored and serious environmental issues are rising as the country continually turns in the way of business. Logging, salmon farming, hydroelectricity projects and mining have led to severe ecological problems.

The bigwigs of the copper industry, which accounts for the majority of the country's economic success, along with the Catholic Church, wield considerable power. To the dismay of the Church, however, the country passed its first divorce law in 2004, and began teaching sex education in schools in 2005.

Truck painted with the Chilean flag in Patagonia

The legacy of Pinochet

The death at the age of 91 of ex-dictator General Augusto Pinochet in late 2006 set a short-lived wave of cheer and clashes between supporters and opponents throughout the country. Many saw his death as cause for celebration, and hundreds turned out in Santiago's plazas to wave flags, drink champagne and throw confetti. Pinochet's supporters also turned out. Efforts had intensified over the past decade to bring him to trial; however, many saw him as immune from the law and thought he would never face justice.

Violence

Pinochet led the US-backed coup against then-president Allende, the world's first democratically elected Socialist leader. During the 11 September 1973 coup, Pinochet and his followers, after storming the Presidential offices of Allende, gathered thousands of people into the national football stadium where they were beaten, tortured or even killed. After the coup, the general found a hole in the power vacuum and gradually gained complete control of the country, dissolved Congress and banned left-wing groups.

Arrested, extradited and charged

Throughout his reign more than 3,000 of his opponents were simply made to disappear, with no trace of them to be found, while tens of thousands more were tortured. The junta lasted for 17 long years until Pinochet was defeated by the voters in an attempt to ratify his presidency until 1997. Yet the army, of which he still had control, retained considerable power and he appointed himself senator in 1997 upon retiring, becoming immune from any charges.

He was arrested in London in September 1998, at the request

The Congreso Nacional in Valparaíso

Army guard outside the presidential offices in Santiago

of a Spanish judge who was investigating the disappearance of Spanish citizens during the 1973 coup, and more than 300 charges were pending at the time of his death. He was extradited to Chile, however, and all charges were thrown out.

Culture

Chile, with its isolated mountains, ocean and desert, began a road to development unique from its neighbours. People are proud of this distinctiveness and anxious to tell you how great their country is, how their fruit is the sweetest and how their wine has won the most international awards.

Coming by air to Santiago, your first impression of Chile will be that it seems just like any European or North American metropolis, but quickly that notion is dismissed. Legions of displaced immigrants and indigenous groups have played their part in shaping the nation. Only rare individuals have been able to tame the wild terrain, which has inspired art and music on a grand scale on the international stage. Two Nobel Prize winners in literature, numerous award-winning classical composers, rock bands, sculptors and a long list of globally famous films have set Chile apart.

New-found freedom

After the return to democracy in 1989, a cultural revolution began and freedom of expression has returned. A move towards a more open and liberal society has begun, with less reliance on the views of the Catholic Church and a general challenge to

conservative values. Homosexuality and divorce are gradually becoming more accepted, while tight-knit families, Christian attitudes and a strong sense of patriotism prevail.

Indigenous cultures

Although the Mapuche have been pushed further and further into the

Inside the Catedral Metropolitana in Santiago

fringes of Chilean society, their influence can still be seen. Hundreds of thousands of Mapuche now populate the streets of Santiago, attempting to find work and integrate into society. However, many of their traditions and values have been brought with them. Many words in Mapudungun have made their way into everyday Chilean vernacular.

Elsewhere, the Aymara that live in the Altiplano along the northern border talk, dress and look more like their neighbours in Peru and Bolivia than those in Chile. In San Pedro de Atacama, Spanish influence is almost completely lost. The atmosphere is entirely Indian, with *adobe* (mud) houses and a mostly native population. Of all of these groups, ceramics, weavings, art and even music have gone mainstream and can be found everywhere from boutique shops to airports.

Woodcarvings combining Christianity with local mythology

Foreign influence

Chileans have always compared themselves not with other Latin American countries, but with European powers such as Britain, who had a role in liberating the country and developing it economically. The Spanish of course have played the biggest hand, but other groups provided their touches as well. German immigration in the Lakes District was encouraged during the mid-19th century to settle the Mapuche heartland and reduce the native population.

Their influence can be seen in the food, art, music and cultural institutions of the area. In Patagonia, street names, politicians and even a TV channel are of Croatian origin. European immigrants such as Welsh, Irish and Croatian settlers came in droves to work the ranches and docks surrounding Punta Arenas, and the population there today heavily reflects this. In the large cities other immigrant groups have begun to appear. Palestinian, Japanese and Korean communities have developed since the 1990s, and migration from Argentina and Peru is also on the increase.

Chile's literary past, present and future

Chile is a country of poets and writers, and they have produced some of the 20th century's best. They have been the rock stars of the country; they are celebrities and are well respected. The literacy rate is more than 94 per cent – among the highest in Latin America – and bookshops and newsstands are plentiful in every town.

Gabriela Mistral (1889–1957), who was born in the Elqui Valley in Vicuña, won South America's first Nobel Prize for literature (1945). Mistral was a shy, rural schoolteacher (and one-time principal of Pablo Neruda at Temuco high school) when she first rose to fame for her poetry, which finds its inspiration in maternal love, in the world of children and the natural environment. *Sonetos de la muerte* (1914), or *Love Poems in Memory of the Dead*, was her first big success. Later collections of poems such as *Desolación* (*Desolation*, 1922) and *Ternura* (*Tenderness*, 1924) are some of her most notable works.

Without question, the national poet is Ricardo Eliecer Neftalí Reyes Basoalto, otherwise known as **Pablo Neruda** (1904–73). No one has better captured the soul and spirit of this

Monument in honour of Gabriela Mistral and Pablo Neruda, two Nobel Prize winners in literature, in Viña del Mar

country quite like him. Romantic, compassionate, humorous, adventurous and thought provoking, he was actively involved in Chilean politics as a senator and a communist, and engaged political debate among Chilean leaders on many occasions. So much so that he was forced into exile in Europe, which is the basis of the 1994 film *Il Postino*, or *The Postman*, by British director Michael Radford.

Neruda grew up in Temuco, but moved when he was a teenager to Santiago and travelled much of the world as a diplomat for the country.

Graffiti sketch of Pablo Neruda on a Bellavista (Santiago) street

Neruda had a number of houses around the country; in Santiago, Valparaíso and Isla Negra, which was stormed as he lay dying of cancer days after the 11 September coup. The houses are now museums where you can see his odd collections of bric-a-brac from his world travels, and paintings and designs by many of his artist friends. His poems have been collected in numerous books and anthologies, and Neruda was awarded the Nobel Prize for literature in 1971.

Isabel Allende (1942–) is the country's most famous contemporary literary figure, although she now lives in the US. She is the niece of former President Salvador Allende and gained fame for her novels, which capture the country in magical realism with a heavy twist of nostalgia. Her works, such as *House of the Spirits*, *Eva Luna* and *My Invented Country* frequent international bestseller lists and several have been adapted into award-winning films.

Other contemporary authors include **Marcela Serrano** (1951–), who is one of the most prolific writers in Latin America today. His work includes *Lo Que Está en Mi Corazón* (*What is in My Heart*, 2002) and *Antigua Vida Mia* (*My Old Life*, 2000). **Pedro Lemebel** (1950–), author of *Tengo Miedo Torero* (*My Tender Matador*), has shaken up Chilean values by writing about homosexuality and other once taboo subjects.

Festivals and events

Festivals are time for Chile's indigenous groups and immigrant populations to show off their traditional culture. Most come with elaborate costumes and all-night music, dancing and drinking. Many are based on Christian or native beliefs, at times combining the two for something uniquely Chilean. Festivals happen all year round, but the best and largest occur during the summer months.

January

Año Nuevo (New Year) Events are held across the country. The largest being the fireworks display in Valparaíso, which attracts hundreds of thousands of visitors to the city and was looked upon each year by Pablo Neruda from his balcony at La Sebastiana. *31 Dec/1 Jan.*

Bierfest Kuntsmann Valdivia (Kuntsmann Beer Festival) Beer festival held near the Cervecería Kuntsmann, celebrating German beer, food and music. *Four days near the end of Jan.*

Semana Ancuditana Cultural festival held across Chiloé, particularly Ancud, celebrating the island's unique music, dance and cuisine. *Second week in January.*

Semana Musica de Frutillar (Music Week in Frutillar) A wide variety of concerts, symphonies and ballets, consisting of various musical genres. *27 January–4 February.*

February

Carnaval Ginga Three-day event in Arica celebrating dancing and music of traditional comparsa groups. *Mid-February.*

Carnaval Putre Altiplano festival days before Lent with lots of music,

Churro stands can be found at nearly every Chilean festival

costumes, masks, disguises and the tossing of flour-filled balloons. The festival culminates in the burning of the *momo*, the symbol of the Carnaval. *February.*

Festival Internacional de la Canción (International Song Festival) One of the biggest music festivals in South America attracts big name acts from across the world to Viña del Mar. *One week in February.*

Noche de Valdivia (Valdivia Night) Held along Valdivia's riverfront, dozens of boats are elaborately decorated like parade floats by teams of families and community groups. Prizes attract crowds of up to 150,000. The night ends with a large fireworks display. *Third Saturday of February.*

Tapati Rapa Nui Annual festival of Rapa Nui culture. Largest festival on the island, with Moai carving, dance, body painting and cultural events. *February.*

Triatlón Internacional de Pucón (Pucón International Triathlon) Large sporting event attracting an international crowd to watch some of the world's best compete in this swimming, cycling and running event. Followed by a night of intense partying. *First week in February.*

March

Campeonato Nacional de Rodeo (National Rodeo Championship) The finals of months of regional championships are held each year in Rancagua. *Late March/early April.*

Fiestas de la Vendimia (Wine Harvest Festival) Held at vineyards across the country. Lively events include grape stomping, beauty pageants, contests, dancing, feasts and of course tastings. *Early March.*

June

Noche de San Juan Festival in Castro, Chiloé, with typical foods, music and dancing heavily laden in mythology. *23 June.*

July

Campeonato Nacional de Surf (National Surf Championship) The best surfers in the country descend upon a selected spot, such as Arica or Pichilemu, on the northern coast. *July.*

Carnaval de Invierno (Winter Carnival) Two-day festival in Punta Arenas with parades and partying to celebrate the start of the winter season. The event culminates in a firework display over the Strait of Magellan. *Last week of July.*

Virgen del Carmen Largest religious event in the country, celebrating the Virgin Mary with costumes, devil masks, dancing and music. Held in La Tirana, east of Iquique, it attracts more than 80,000 people each year. *Mid-July.*

September

Fiestas Patrias (Independence Day Celebrations) The country celebrates with parades, festivities, food, music, dancing and heavy drinking in *ramadas* (open-air buildings). *18 September.*

Highlights

Page

28	Santiago
42	Norte Grande & Norte Chico
62	Central Chile
76	Lakes District
90	Chiloé
98	Northern Patagonia
106	Southern Patagonia

1 Parque Nacional Lauca
The park combines the most incredible sights of the Chilean Altiplano with traditional Aymara villages, thriving culture, volcanoes and herds of camelids.

2 San Pedro de Atacama
An *adobe* (mud) paradise converted to one of the world's top backpacker hangouts. Endless opportunities to explore the surrounding countryside filled with salt flats, volcanoes and geysers.

3 Portillo ski resort Posh, expensive and filled with beautiful people and some of the world's best skiers, Portillo is the paramount ski resort in South America.

4 Chilean vineyards Once thought to offer just Merlot, in the last decade it was discovered that Chile held some of the world's last pure Carmenère vines, which thrive in the valleys south of Santiago and have revolutionised the wine industry, specifically in places such as the Colchagua and Maipú valleys.

5 Santiago's café/dining scene
Enjoy the cuisine at some of the pavement cafés in Bellavista or the posh Providencia bistros and fine-dining establishments along Avenida Providencia.

6 Valparaíso Ascensors climb steep hills lined with houses built in Valpo's own unique style, which is brilliantly romantic and also a UNESCO World Heritage Site.

7 Chiloé Unlike anywhere else in the world, the Chiloé archipelago is full of mist and legend. Tales tell of *brujos* (witches) who push islanders away from their clean, Christian lives.

8 The Lakes District German influence is met by that of the indigenous Mapuche and spread across a region filled with forest-, lake- and volcano-covered national parks.

9 Chilean fiords Seen only by multiple-day boat trips, Chile's fiords pass some of the world's largest ice fields and glaciers.

10 Parque Nacional Torres del Paine Perhaps the world's most stunning natural park and home to eye-catching scenery in every direction.

Highlights

Suggested itineraries

Where to go

What you will see in Chile heavily relies on both the season and the amount of time you have. Weather changes are increasingly more dramatic from north to south and the country is so long and so diverse, that you could spend months travelling and still not see a fraction of what the country holds. There is a wide range of itineraries available. Here are just a few:

One week

Considering the long distance most travel to reach the country, weekend stays are very rare, therefore staying for at least a week is essential. As nearly everyone flies directly into Santiago, most will explore the cultural delights of the capital and the coastal cities of Valparaíso, Viña del Mar and Isla Negra. Santiago also sits within driving distance of two of the country's major activities: wine tasting and skiing. Many come specifically for the wine routes, such as the Colchagua or Maule Valley, and spend each day visiting a different vineyard or relaxing at one of the many vineyard spas. Visits to ski resorts such as Portillo are often oriented around week-long stays.

Two weeks

The arrival of low cost air carriers has made seeing many parts of the country much more affordable and easy to reach. Most travellers will land in Santiago and explore the surrounding

Concha y Toro vineyard outside of Santiago

Lago Pehoé and lodge in Parque Nacional Torres del Paine

area and take one connecting flight or long bus trip to another region, such as Southern Patagonia, the Lakes District or the Northen Grande. In Southern Patagonia, Torres del Paine is the highlight of most trips and one of the most popular destinations on the continent. A number of activities can be done in and around the park, and many stay for several weeks. For instance, the 'W' hike will take a full five days, while the circuit will take a week and a half. Rafting, kayaking and horse riding trips can take days as well. The highlights of the park can be seen on a day tour, however. The Lakes District has countless national parks and stunning natural sites and numerous resort towns have sprung up across the region. For most, they will pick just one or two towns and stick to those. However, you could spend months exploring this region. The Norte Grande is fairly spread out and trips other than by plane are long. A

quick tour could last about a week and take you to the major highlights of the Parque Nacional Lauca and San Pedro de Atacama.

Longer visits

Many combine visits to Chile with trips to Peru, Bolivia or Argentina, flying into Santiago and out of Lima or Buenos Aires, or vice versa, travelling overland in between.

Some of the best sights in the country are quite isolated and cannot be appreciated without significant time. Most will combine many of the itineraries above with trips to isolated locations, such as the island of Chiloé and the smaller surrounding islands in the archipelago or ferry trips through Chile's glacier-filled fiords. Options include a flight to the Americas' most southerly point of land at Isla Navarino or to Chile's foothold on Antarctica, as well as excursions across the border into Argentina.

Santiago

With more than six million people populating Chile's capital, one's first impressions of the country are often completely different from those of the rest of the country. Towering skyscrapers, a modern metro system and shops featuring top international designers are paired with 500-year-old colonial buildings and leafy green parks.

The scars of the past are slowly fading and a free trade agreement with the US in 2003, has led to the city's materialisation as a global business hub, putting money in the city's pockets and leading to a construction boom with new hotels and some of the finest restaurants on the continent. Once one of the most polluted cities in the world and covered in a haze of smog due to the thousands of diesel-pumping buses that covered every street, Santiago's public transport system has been completely overhauled. It has been one of the biggest transformations of any Latin American city.

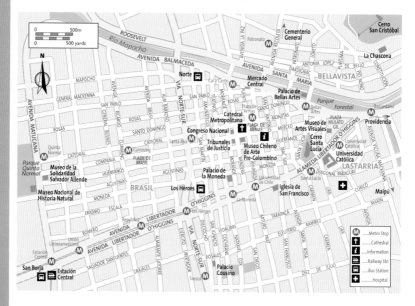

Santiago urban sprawl as seen from Cerro San Cristóbal

The city was founded as Santiago de la Nueva Extremadura, by the Spanish conquistador Pedro de Valdivia in 1541, who arrived after an 11-month journey from Cusco. It remained a small settlement until the middle of the 19th century, when the California gold rush caused the number of exports to rise substantially and the population to swell to more than 100,000. Over the next 100 years, industrialisation caused poverty in the countryside and an influx of Chileans moved to the cities, many in squatter settlements that literally sprung up overnight. Now the city sprawls outwards in every direction, straddling the Río Mapocho and butting up against Cerro Santa Lucía. The beautiful backdrop of the Cordillera of the Andes watches over the city, roughly divided into two: the affluent eastern suburbs called the *Barrios* Altos and the poor settlements to the south.

Although intimidating at first, you will quickly find that the central part of the city is easily navigable and much of it can be done on foot.

Tourist Information: SERNATUR

Av Providencia 1550, Second floor, Providencia, Santiago. Tel: 2-731-8419. www.sernatur.cl. Open: Mon–Fri 8.45am–6.30pm, Sat 9am–2pm.
The country's national tourism office is located in between the Manuel Montt and Pedro de Valdivia metro stations. There is also an office at the airport and municipal tourist offices (*www.ciudad.cl*) located around town at Merced 860, just off the Plaza and Providencia 2359, in Providencia.

SANTIAGO NEIGHBOURHOODS

Santiago is divided into 32 different districts or *barrios*, each with its own unique characteristics and atmosphere. Most visitors flutter through the city in a day or so, but if you have the time, the magic of the city can be found drifting slowly in and out of pavement cafés, *barrio* by *barrio*.

The new metro system has drastically improved getting around the city and new routes are opening each month. Most of the stations are small and easy to get around and will usually connect to no more than one other line.
Open: Mon–Sat 6.30am–10.30pm, Sun 8am–10.30pm. Tickets cost: $380 pesos for off-peak times, and $420 pesos for peak times (7–9am & 6–8pm).

Centro Histórico (Historic Centre)

Santiago's colonial centre is spread on a triangular-shaped grid between the Río Mapocho in the north, the Alameda to the south and the Vía Norte Sur to the west. The area is a mishmash of old and modern, where stone churches sit beside contemporary glass buildings, radiating from the palm-lined Plaza de Armas. The Catedral Metropolitana and the Museo Histórico Nacional surround monuments, statues, art sales and strolling musicians on the colonial square. A number of pedestrian shopping centres are filled with shops, banks and the city's trademark *cafés con piernas* (coffee on legs) – essentially, coffeeshops behind mirrored windows with scantily clad waitresses. Note the

architecture of Luciano Kulczewski. The Gaudí-like artist designed many of the art nouveau houses and gargoyles and ironwork.
Metro: Plaza de Armas.

Barrio Bellavista

After the 1973 coup, many of the country's artists were forced to flee the city, but after the restoration of democracy in 1990, they began to return, and nowhere is this more evident than Bellavista, the city's Bohemian district, located north of the centre and the Río Mapocho. This is where Pablo Neruda had a house (now a museum). The *barrio* is filled with galleries and craft shops. It's the centre of the city's café culture and also has many lively bars and restaurants, drawing a flood of visitors until dawn on weekend nights.
Reached by Baquedano metro station and then by crossing the Río Mapocho.

Barrio Brasil

Often ignored in the recent past, this once élite neighbourhood west of the centre has been redeveloped by a number of younger Santiaguinos looking to enjoy the lower rents and artsy kicks. Fashionable restaurants and clubs have returned, invigorating the atmosphere. A monkey puzzle tree on Plaza de Brasil is the centre of the neighbourhood, both physically and culturally, as it becomes a lively hangout on weekend nights. The cobblestone streets of *Barrio* Concha y

Toro, now swallowed by *Barrio* Brasil, retains much of the colonial charm lost in the rest of the area.
Barrio *Brasil is west of the Vía Norte Sur. Metro: República.*

Barrio **Lastarria**

This is one of the most central districts and is characterised by its broad avenues and leafy streets. These are lined with Parisian-style buildings filled with hotels, pavement cafés and great bars. The *barrio* is home to the Universidad Católica, as well as numerous theatres and museums. For mid-range accommodation, there isn't a better option as you are within walking distance to nearly every attraction or nightlife spot.

East of the centre, before Parque General Bustamante. Metro: Baquedano, Universidad Católica or Bellas Artes.

Bellas Artes

This section of the centre is defined by the Palacio de Bellas Artes, the home of two of the best art museums in the country. The area has become a hip alternative to Providencia or Bellavista, as bars and restaurants spring up each day alongside many of the city's best theatres. A Saturday flea market on Plaza Mulato Gil is a great place to find a number of antiques such as jewellery, books and various trinkets. *Parque Forestal, José Miguel de la Barra. Metro: Bellas Artes.*

Cafés and restaurants in Bellavista

Mercado Central (Central Market)

This lively market offers just about any kind of seafood as the daily catches are brought in from the coast. The central glass and wrought-iron enclosed courtyard, built by the British, has tuxedo-clad waiters beckoning you to one of the tables of the many restaurants. Arrive early to see the fish being unloaded and local restaurateurs scrambling for the best pieces.

The Mercado Central is just south of the Parque Venezuela or three blocks north of the Plaza de Armas. Metro: Puente Cal y Canto.

Catedral Metropolitana

Providencia

The residential and commercial area is one of the most sophisticated. Home to many of the social élite, as well as the most expensive restaurants, clubs and hotels, it lacks attractions, though most visitors are content to just enjoy the bounties of being in a cosmopolitan city. Leafy side streets contain some of Santiago's finest dining, while the noisy centre, Avenida Providencia, is where most of the shopping, hotels and metro stops can be found.

Northeast of the centre, south of the Río Mapocho. Metro: Manuel Montt or Pedro de Valdivia.

GARDENS, PARKS, MUSEUMS AND VINEYARDS
Gardens, parks and museums
Catedral Metropolitana

Dominating the Plaza de Armas, this cathedral was designed in the mid-18th century by German architects Hagen and Vogel, but a few decades later remodelled by Italian architect Toesca. It is one of the largest churches in the country, with lavish altars, some of which are set in lapis lazuli.

Plaza de Armas. Open: Mon–Sat 9am–7pm, Sun 9am–noon.

Cementerio General

The tombs of many of Chile's most prominent citizens can be found here, including Salvador Allende as well as many other presidents and political heroes, such as José Manuel Balmaceda. The massive tombs form a small city of

sorts, featuring an array of architecture. A wall of memory is dedicated to the victims of the Pinochet years, more than a thousand of which were seemingly 'disappeared' from the face of the earth, with no record of their deaths.
Avenida Recoleta. Tel: 2-737-9469. Open: daily during daylight hours. Metro: Cementerio General.

Cerro San Cristóbal

For views of the entire Santiago metropolitan area this mountain is the place. The recreation area, also known as Parque Metropolitano, is home to the Virgen de Inmaculada Concepción, which towers over the city from the peak at 860m (2822ft). A small chapel sits just below, where the late Pope John Paul II gave mass during his 1984 visit. There are a number of terraces from which to admire the city or have a snack, as well as several of the city's best swimming pools and a small zoo.
Reached by funicular (Open: Mon 1–8pm, Tue–Sun 10am–8pm) from Bellavista or a teleferiqo (aerial tramway) (Open: Mon 2.30–6.30pm, Tue–Fri noon–6.30pm, Sat 10.30am–7.30pm) from Providencia. Admission charge.

Cerro Santa Lucía

This green space on a small hill was transformed in the late 19th century by Mayor Benjamín Vicuña Mackenna (whose tomb lies near the summit) from a rocky wasteland to a landscaped park boasting panoramic views.
The park, open during daylight hours, sits along the Alameda between Subercaseaux and Santa Lucía.

La Chascona

Pablo Neruda's Santiago home overlooks the city from the foot of Cerro San Cristóbal in Bellavista. Named after the hair of his third wife, Matilde, the ship-shaped house is filled with Neruda's collections of items such as mastheads, carvings, Bauhaus furniture and books. There's also a café and gift shop.
From the Baquedano metro station, cross the river and head north ten minutes to Fernando Márquez de la Plata 192. Tel: 2-777-8741. www.fundacionneruda.org. Open: Tue–Sun 10am–6pm. Admission charge.

Iglesia de San Francisco/ Museo Colonial

The centrepiece of this 16th-century church is the carved image of the Virgen del Socorro carried by Pedro de Valdivia, buried here, on his travels. The image is thought to have protected the *mudejar*-style church from numerous earthquakes. The museum has a large collection of religious art, mostly from the Cuzco school.
Located on the Alameda near the Universidad de Chile metro station. Church: Open: Mon–Sat 11am–6pm, Sun 10am–1pm. Museum: Open: Tue–Sat 10am–1pm & 3–6pm, Sun 10am–2pm. Admission charge.

Museo de Artes Visuales (Museum of Visual Arts)

MAVI is the centre for Chilean contemporary art and showcases the work of more than 300 artists. Exhibits of sculpture, photography, engravings and paintings rotate frequently. The small but interesting Museo Arqueológico de Santiago sits next door.

Lastarria 307, at Plaza Mulato Gil de Castro, two blocks east of the Bellas Artes Metro station. Tel: 2-664-9337. www.mavi.cl. Open: Tue–Sun 10.30am–6pm. Admission charge.

Museo Chileno de Arte Pre-Colombino

This museum looks at pre-Colombian artefacts as art – and the result is incredible. Pieces are divided by culture, and range from weavings of coastal Peru and Chile, Chinchorro mummies (*see pp46–7*), intricate gold and silver work and Mapuch woodcarvings.

Bandera 361, one block from the Plaza de Armas. Tel: 2-688-77348. www.precolombino.cl. Open: Tue–Sat 10am–6pm, Sun 10am–2pm. Admission charge. Metro: Plaza de Armas.

Museo de la Solidaridad Salvador Allende

The museum in this restored colonial mansion was built in honour of Allende and the socialist movement. When the Pinochet regime took power, the collection of more than 400 pieces was hidden in the basement of the Museum of Modern Art. The pieces are from many of the biggest names in the 20th century, including Miró, Tapies and even Yoko Ono.

Herrera 360 in Barrio Brasil. Tel: 2-689-8761. www.mssa.cl. Open: Tue–Sun 9am–1pm. Admission charge. Metro: Unión Latinoamericana.

Palacio de Bellas Artes

Based on the Petit Palais in Paris, this beautiful neo-classical palace in Parque Forestal is split into two museums:
José Miguel de la Barra, just north of the Bellas Artes metro station in Parque Forestal.

Museo de Arte Contemporáneo

This half of the palace underwent a $3 million expansion that included the restoration of a Belgian cupola damaged in a 1969 fire. Contemporary displays of photography, video imaging and sculptures are paired with a library and archive run by the Universidad de Chile's art department.

Tel: 2-639-6488. www.mac.uchile.cl. Open: Tue–Sat 11am–7pm, Sun 11am–5pm. Admission charge.

Museo Nacional de Bellas Artes

Rivalled only by Palacio Vergara in Viña del Mar, this museum holds the country's greatest art collection. The museum houses 2,700 pieces of mostly European works, as well as some Chilean. There are occasional international exhibitions.

Tel: 2-633-4472. Open: Tue–Sun 10am–6.30pm. Admission charge.

Palacio Cousiño

Built on the wealth of wine and silver mining, this is one of the most elaborate mansions in Chile. Built in 1871 by the French architect Paul Lathoud on the orders of the Cousiño-Goyenechea family, the mansion, which is a national monument, is filled with French art, period furniture, parquet floors, velvets and porcelain from Sèvres. It is sectioned off into 12 rooms including a weapons room and golden room, the site of many great balls.
South of the Alameda, just beside the Vía Norte Sur. www.palaciocousino.cl. Open: Tue–Fri 9.30am–1.30pm & 2.30–5pm, Sat–Sun 9.30am–1.30pm. Admission charge. Metro: Toesca.

Palacio de la Moneda

These 200-year-old neo-classical presidential offices designed by Italian architect Joaquín Toesca are one of the most significant historic locations in the entire country. This is where General Augusto Pinochet staged his 1973 coup. President Salvador Allende gave his last words over a radio address here, just before an apparent suicide. Much of the building was damaged by air force raids during the coup, but has

Cerro Santa Lucía gives views of Santiago from its many tree-lined paths and terraces

since been refurbished. A changing of the guard ceremony occurs at 10am on even-numbered days.
Between Plaza de la Constitución and the Alameda, Morandé 130. Tel: 2-690-4000. www.presidencia.cl. Open: Mon–Fri 10am–6pm. Call a day in advance for reservations. Metro: La Moneda.

Parque de las Esculturas
This sculpture park covers 21,500sq m (231,432sq ft) along the Río Mapocho, a restoration of an area that was destroyed when the river burst its banks in 1982. The park flaunts a number of native tree species mixed with post-modern sculptures from well-known Chilean artists.
Providencia, between the Río Mapocho and Av Santa Maria.

Parque Quinta Normal
This 40-ha (99-acre) park (*Open: Tue–Sun 8am–8.30pm. Metro: Quinta Normal*) beside the Universidad de Santiago is set in an exclusive residential area filled with mansions. The highlights are the handful of museums that dot the park, but on a given day you will find numerous joggers, *futbolistas* (footballers) and picnickers. The **Museo Nacional de Historia Natural** (*Tel: 2-681-4095. Open: Tue–Sun 10am–5.30pm. Admission charge*), which contains bone fragments of a Milodón – a giant ground sloth found in a cave near Puerta Natales – is the most important

of the museums in the park. Elsewhere, the **Museo Artequín** (*Tel: 2-681-8687. Open: Tue–Fri 9am–5pm, Sat–Sun 11am–6pm. Admission charge*) was the Chilean Pavilion of the Paris Exhibition in 1889, which was shipped back to Santiago in pieces and then reconstructed. It now houses recreations of European works.

Templo Votivo de Maipú
This temple houses the ruins of the original earthquake-damaged temple and the reconstructed one. It is set on the site of the battle of **Maipú** where the final battle between Chile and Spain took place, and honours Virgen del Carmen, who is said to have lifted the Chilean army in victory.
Carmen 1750 in Maipú, 45 minutes from the centre. You can catch a southbound metro bus called Templo from Av Vicuña Mackenna. Tel: 2-531-2312. Open: 9am–8pm. Free admission.

Vineyards
Viña Concha y Toro
Due to its easy access to the city, beautifully landscaped gardens and refurbished colonial buildings, this is one of the most visited wineries in the country. Tours in both English and Spanish are frequent and well organised, and include generous samples and a beautiful café/bar. The eerie basement cellar, known as Casillero del Diabolo, or the Devil's Cellar, was so named by the founder to scare off locals who kept stealing the wine.

Pirque. Go to the Bellavista de la Florida metro stop and hop on a southbound metro bus across the street from the station. Arrange the tour a day in advance during the summer (Tel: 2-476-5669. www.conchaytoro.com). Many tour companies can arrange the entire excursion from Santiago. Tours: Mon–Fri 11.30am & 3pm, Sat 10am & noon. Admission charge.

Viña Cousiño Macul

Located just outside the city, this winery is one of the few in the country that is still run by the original founding family. Their cellar, built 6m (20ft) underground in 1872 by French architects, is considered one of the oldest and finest in Chile. The 45-minute tours take you through the winemaking process and are followed by tastings of one reserve and one varietal wine.
Peñalolén, southeast of the centre. Take a No 390 bus from the Alameda. Tel: 2-351-4175. www.cousinomacul.cl. Tours: Mon–Fri 11am & 3pm, Sat 11am. Admission charge.

Viña de Martino

This family-operated vineyard, with 400ha (988 acres) on a beautiful setting directly between the Andes and the Pacific, grows Cabernet Sauvignon, Merlot, Carmenère, Malbec, Sauvignon Blanc, Chardonnay and Semillón. It's one of the more contemporary vineyards, and is one of the first in the country to delve into organic wines. Bilingual guides lead you through the vinification process and allow you to sample their Tuscan-style vinoteca. They arrange tours with lunches in the vineyard, and access to as much Reserve wine as you care to drink.
In Isla del Maipo, approximately one hour southwest of the centre by bus from Terminal San Borja. Tel: 2-819-2062. www.demartino.cl. Tours: Mon–Sat noon. Admission charge.

Casillero del Diabolo, the famous cellar at Viña Concha y Toro

Walk: Central Santiago

Although it is a city of six million, it's easily navigable and the major highlights of the centre can be seen in just under a day.

*Begin at Plaza Vicuña Mackenna, walking along the Alameda, across from the Santa Lucía metro stop. From here, walk up the steps to the top of **Cerro Santa Lucía** to enjoy the landscaped park, Japanese gardens and morning view over the centre. If you want to save your legs, there is an* ascensor *or lift at the northern end of the hill.*

1 After making your way down, move west along the Alameda to **Iglesia de San Francisco**, the city's oldest colonial building and home to the revered image of the Virgen de Socorro. The **Museo Colonial** inside is one of the

best places in the world to see religious art from the Cuzqueña school.

2 Move just a few blocks west on the Alameda then turn right onto Av Morandé, where you will find the

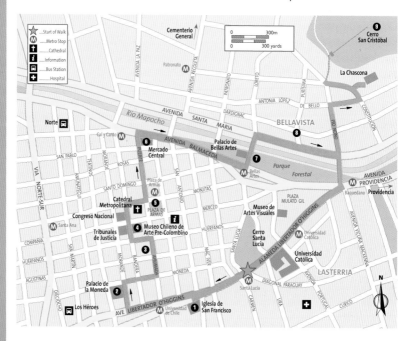

Palacio de la Moneda, the presidential offices and the site of the 1973 coup by General Augusto Pinochet. Designed by Italian architect Joaquín Toesca, the building was originally a mint, and you can tour the inside if you book a day or so in advance.

3 Keep walking along Morandé and turn right at the next corner and then left onto **Paseo Ahumada**, a pedestrian-only street where you can stop for a coffee in one of the many *cafés con piernas* (coffee on legs). Turn left at Paseo Huérfanos, before heading right at Bandera, where you'll pass the **Tribunales de Justicia**.

4 One of the most interesting museums in the country can be found here as well: **Museo Chileno de Arte Pre-Colombino**. Continue up Bandera, past the former home of the **Congreso Nacional**, then turn right at Monjitas, which leads to the **Plaza de Armas**, a block away.

5 The palm-shaded plaza is one of the best people-watching opportunities in

Central Santiago

the city. Here you will also find the neo-classical **Catedral Metropolitana**, designed by Toesca, who also did the **Palacio de la Moneda**, and the **Museo Histórico Nacional**, which house artefacts from Chile's colonial and republican eras.

Walk north three blocks along Paseo Puente to the **Mercado Central** for lunch.

6 The restaurants in the central, stained-glass enclosed courtyard, serve just about any type of seafood, but opt for Chilean specialities such as *pailla marina* (seafood stew).

7 After lunch take a leisurely stroll east through the **Parque Forestal** to the **Palacio Bellas Artes**, where you will find two art museums with one of the best overall collections of European and national art in the country.

8 For the rest of the afternoon, cross the Río Mapocho to **Bellavista**, the city's bohemian quarter, and wander through the shady streets, hopping in and out of galleries, eventually stopping at the Santiago home of Pablo Neruda, **La Chascona**, at the foot of Cerro San Cristóbal.

9 From here take the funicular up the hill to the top of **Cerro San Cristóbal**, where, if the day is clear and the light is good, you should be able to capture the perfect image of the whole of the city and surrounding mountains.

Excursion: Cajón del Maipo

The Río Maipo Canyon, wedged between the capital and the Andes, is the largest recreational area near the city and the first choice for Santiaguinos to get away from the smog and noise of the crowded streets. It's the home of a national park and reserve, volcanoes, hot springs, lodges, abundant camping facilities and even vineyards. Even though it can be reached from the city in an hour, endless excursions can be made by biking, white-water rafting, hiking and skiing. The scenery ranges from dusty brown desert scattered with cacti and high grasses of the pampas, to the glaciers and snow-covered peaks of the Cordillera. Condors and other rare birds can be seen flying overhead, while small lizards scurry below.

1 The **Monumento Natural El Morado** is perhaps the most stunning site in the canyon. Although small with just 5,000ha (12,355 acres), it holds the 5,060m (16,601ft) El Morado mountain and has stunning views of the San Francisco and El Morado glaciers. One of the most popular hikes takes two hours from the hot springs of Baños Morales and brings you to the glistening mountain lake, Laguna Morales, where the San Francisco

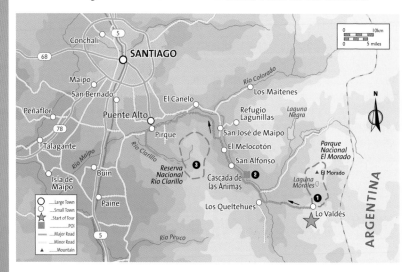

glacier is best spotted. Many Santiaguinos come for the weekend to camp or go horse riding.

The park is 93km (58 miles) from Santiago, reachable by bus from the Bellavista de la Florida Metro station. Open: Nov–Apr. Admission charge.

2 Originally a horse ranch, the **Cascada de las Ánimas** is a 3,500ha (8,648-acre) private reserve that has been run by the bohemian Astorga-Moreno family since 1840. It is set among forests and has amazingly beautiful views of the Andes. Set on the banks of the raging Río Maipo, it is named after a waterfall found within. It is located in San Alfonso, 60km (37 miles) from Santiago and is the most developed in the canyon, with a charming hostel, hot springs, massage facilities, meditation, yoga and an excellent restaurant. This is the place to come for rafting and organised treks. Rapids are mostly Class III and pass the grounds of Pinochet's former estate at El Melocotón, where a nearby rapid has been nicknamed 'El Pinocho'. The reserve is also a working horse ranch where riding is available from a few hours to two weeks.

Tel: 2-861-1303. www.cascada.net. You can get to the reserve from a Cajón del Maipo marked bus, from the Bellavista de la Florida metro station. Open: daily 8.30am–8pm. Admission charge.

3 The **Reserva Nacional Río Clarillo**, near Pirque, covers an area of 13,185ha

Cactus in the canyon, typical plant of area

(32,580 acres), at an altitude climbing from 850m (2,789ft) to 3,500m (11,483ft). This is one of the best parts of the canyon to appreciate its diverse flora and fauna including the peumo, litre, lun and quillay sclerophyllous trees and the endangered Chilean woodpecker and Chilean iguana. A number of hiking trails take you deep within the reserve through densely covered forests and strange rock formations.

The reserve can be reached by bus (which will only go as far as 4km/2½ miles from the entrance) or private car from Pirque. www.cajondelmaipo.com. Open: daily 8.30am–6pm. Admission charge.

Norte Grande and Norte Chico

Regions I, II, III and IV, otherwise known as the Norte Grande and Norte Chico, take on a character very different from the rest of the country. No more are there green hills, but here sits dry desert, sand dunes as tall as skyscrapers, astronomical observatories, salt flats, ghost towns and some of the world's oldest mummified human remains that have been perfectly preserved by the arid climate. Much of it takes on the characteristics of neighbouring Peru and Bolivia, of which it was once a part until the War of the Pacific (1879–84).

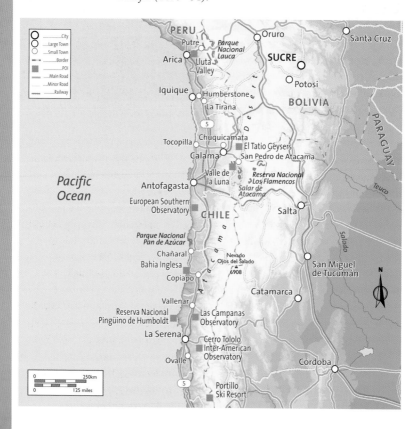

Camping on a beach in the Norte Grande

The Norte Grande and Norte Chico have long been economic powerhouses of the country, with nitrate deposits in the desert used for fertiliser and synthetic alternatives propelling the country forward in the early 20th century as international investors built railways, transfiguring the country's infrastructure. When the nitrate boom ended, the nearby copper mines were waiting to take their place and are still one of the leading factors driving the economy today.

The region is home to the driest desert in the world, the Atacama, which begins here and stretches north along the coast all the way until Tumbes on the Peru–Ecuador border. The Atacama, in parts so dry that nothing grows, has moments of inspiration brought on by sporadic heavy rainfall, where the *desierto florido* (flowering desert) occurs. Land that was nothing more than dirt becomes filled with millions of rare and exotic wildflowers. The Inca influence here is undeniable in places, particularly in the Altiplano on the northern borders, where the dress and architecture takes on a different look and farmers still tend to land on stone terraces as they have done for hundreds of years.

PARQUE NACIONAL LAUCA, PUTRE AND ARICA

Parque Nacional Lauca

This world biosphere reserve near the Bolivian border encompasses much of the Chilean Altiplano, with volcanoes and mineral-rich mountain lakes. It feels like a place in Peru or Bolivia, with Aymara-speaking people chewing coca leaves and making handicrafts and weavings with designs reminiscent of the Incas. Small, Aymara villages such as Parinacota give glimpses into life that has been unchanged for hundreds of years and can be found nowhere else in Chile.

Much of the park sits about 3,200m (10,500ft) above sea level, although several peaks climb to more than 6,300m (20,669ft). Many visitors are left breathless and are overcome by soroche (altitude sickness) on day trips here from sea-level Arica. Most tour companies are now equipped with oxygen tanks.

The park supports a wide variety of wildlife such as vicuña, guanaco, fox, Chilean flamingos, condors and the rabbit-like vizcacha, as well as the domesticated alpaca and llama. There is extensive bird life along the shores of Lago Cotacotani and the other highland bodies of water.

Lago Chungará (4,500m/14,764ft) is often the end point of many trips to the park. It is one of the highest-altitude lakes in the world and its spectacular location at the foot of the dormant Pallachata twin volcanoes of Parinacota and Pomerape makes it the crowning jewel of the park.

Parque Nacional Lauca is located 160km (100 miles) northeast of Arica, reachable by bus or tour from Arica on the La Paz road. Admission charge.

Arica

The dry, sunny port city of Arica maintains a tropical climate, which attracts many tourists who visit its plethora of beaches. It's one of the best surf spots in Chile and has attracted international attention, particularly for the tubes in July, which bring surfers and film crews from around the world to Playa Las Machas, El Gringo and El Buey.

Pre-Colombian petroglyphs at the Museo Arqueológico near Arica

Aymara church in Parinacota

The city is crowned by El Morro, the cape at the southern end, with its enormous statue of Christ.
Arica is located 18km (11 miles) south of the border with Peru on the PanAmerican Highway.

Putre

This 3,530m (11,581ft) Aymara village was originally intended to be a Spanish *reducción*, a Spanish settlement used to 'reduce' the native population. Oddly enough it has had the opposite effect and is now a centre of Aymara culture in Chile.
Putre is 150km (93 miles) east of Arica en route to Parque Nacional Lauca.

Museo Arqueológico San Miguel de Azapa

Built around a centuries old Spanish olive grove and press, this excellent museum has a collection of weavings, carvings and other artefacts from excavations in the Lluta Valley. There is a small display of the Chinchorro mummies (*see pp46–7*) and a garden of petroglyphic boulders found in the Azapa Valley.
The park is located 12km (7½ miles) east of Arica by taxi. Open: Jan–Feb daily 10am–7pm, Mar–Dec daily 10am–6pm. Admission charge.

EIFFEL IN CHILE

In Arica the cast-iron gothic church, Iglesia San Marcos, was designed by Alexandre Gustave Eiffel (of Eiffel Tower fame). Eiffel also designed the Aduana de Arica customhouse near the harbour at Plaza Baquedano. The buildings were ordered by the Peruvian president of the time, who commissioned Eiffel to design projects all over the country. *Open: 9am–2pm & 6–8pm. Free admission.*

Chinchorro mummies

Discovered in the arid desert in southern Peru and northern Chile, the Chinchorro mummies are the oldest known artificially preserved human remains on earth, several millennia older than those of Egypt. The process was begun as far back as 5,000 years by small groups of fishermen, hunters and gatherers, and was incredibly elaborate for what many considered to be a very simple culture.

The mummification process evolved over thousands of years. The black mummies were first and were the most complex. The head and limbs were first dismembered and the bodies reassembled using sticks. Internal organs were replaced with clay, camelid fibres and dried plants. The skull would be cut in half and the brain extracted, then tied back together. Muscles were recreated with thin bundles of wild reeds and sea grasses. Then the skin would be sewn together with plant fibres, with sea lion carcass replacing any holes. The entire body was then covered with an ash paste and finished with a coat of shiny black manganese. A clay mask often covered the face.

The red mummies came next, appearing around 3000 BC. Similarly, the bodies were painted, but this time using red ochre. Most wore clay masks with open eyes and carefully modelled facial features with designs of sexual organs. Wigs of human hair up to 0.6m (2ft) in length were sometimes found on the mummies. The bodies were not completely dismembered, but the head was removed and the brain extracted. Neat incisions were made to remove muscles and intestines.

Mud mummies, which date to 1700 BC, were also found. The process was not nearly as sophisticated. The bodies were simply covered with a thin layer of mud and then encased in a mud paste several centimetres thick.

The Chinchorro left no written explanation of why they practised this act, so scientists can only assume at this point. Various pre-Colombian civilisations believed that death marked a period of transition, rather than the end of life, and that the souls of the deceased should be cared for to ease their journey to the afterlife. In exchange for the hospitality, many believed that they would be ensured fertility and good harvests. They were a vital link between life on earth and the spirit

Chinchorro mummy of a child in a glass case

world. Many of the mummies seem to have been painted many times, which leads scientists to believe that they must have been brought out for celebrations on different occasions. The mummification practice died out sometime around 2,000 BC, although similar practices were adopted by the Incas, who often preserved their rulers and then paraded them around during festivities, to the horror of the Spanish when they arrived.

So far some several hundred Chinchorro mummies have been found; roughly half have gone through the elaborate mummification process described above, while the others were simply preserved by the arid desert. All ages, both sexes and those from every social class have been mummified. The Chinchorro seemingly honoured all humans equally, from nobility to stillborn infants. They can be seen in archaeology museums throughout the country, including the Museo Arqueológico San Miguel de Azapa (see p45) east of Arica and the Museo Chileno de Arte Pre-Colombino in Santiago (see p34).

IQUIQUE AND ENVIRONS
Humberstone

Chilean writer Isabel Allende said that by just hearing the words 'ghost town' in reference to the ones around Iquique '…gave wings to her imagination'. This ghost town had a short history. In 1872 it was built to house the workers employed to process the largest deposit of saltpetre (potassium nitrate) in the world and it was a hub of activity for the next 70 years. With the development of synthetic nitrates, however, the town dwindled down to nearly nothing.

Many of the buildings lay decrepit and crumbling, and machinery lay rusting from the salt blown in from the sea. However, Humberstone was named a UNESCO World Heritage Site in 2005 and restorations have been ongoing. *Humberstone is located 45km (28 miles) east of Iquique. Open: 9am–6.30pm. Admission charge.*

Iquique

Named after the Aymara word for rest and tranquility, the bustling port of Iquique is one of Chile's premier beach resorts. It is blessed with warm weather for much of the year and a surge of recent development has included a glitzy casino and high-rise apartment blocks. A boardwalk runs through the centre of town from the Plaza de Armas, past cafés and colonial buildings, to the coast and along the beach to the south of the centre. Sand dunes tower over the city and are a popular launching spot for paragliders, who ride the air currents that follow the coast.

The city's heyday was during the first quarter of the 20th century, when the

Playa Cavancha in Iquique, one of Chile's premier beaches

Old mill in Humberstone

Huantajaya silver mine was discovered nearby, and minerals and nitrates were shipped by railway through the town. Throughout the city, barons built decadent Georgian mansions. The establishment of the Zona Franca, or duty free zone, in 1975 made Iquique one of Chile's wealthiest cities. Iquique is located 330km (205 miles) south of the Peruvian border and 1,850km (1,150 miles) north of Santiago.

Lluta Valley

The barren valley just north of Arica is best known for the handful of pre-Colombian geoglyphs that lie on the hillsides. These stone patterns were built between AD 1000–1400 and depict eagles, llamas and humans. The largest is El Pájaro, the parrot, at 33km (20¹/₂ miles) wide, although most are no bigger than a few dozen metres. *Located on Highway 11, just east of the PanAmerican Highway.*

La Tirana

This small village is named after an Inca princess, nicknamed the tyrant, who was buried here after escaping from Diego de Almagro during his travels south into Chile. After leaving Almagro, she gathered a group of loyal Inca warriors to attack as many Spaniards or baptised indigenous people as they could find. Later, however, she fell in love with a Portuguese miner who she saved from execution. When she decided to convert to his Christian faith, they were both killed. A cult with hundreds of chapters in northern Chile has evolved around this tale. The city is also host to the ten-day, Virgen del Carmen festival each July (*see p23*), and attracts more than 80,000 costumed pilgrims who come to pay homage to an image of the Virgin. *La Tirana is 72km (45 miles) east of Iquique.*

CHUQUICAMATA
Calama

As the price of copper has risen steadily in recent years, the mining town of Calama has grown in importance. Reminders of the links to the copper industry are everywhere, from the copper-plated spire atop the cathedral, to copper statues and the bus loads of mine workers who shuffle through its streets. The Battle of Calama in 1879, which took place across the Río Loa, marked the start of the War of the Pacific.

Calama is reached by air or bus from Santiago and Antofagasta.

Chuquicamata

The site of the actual mine is enormous and the hole that has been made in

Chuquicamata coppper mine

Massive earth-moving vehicles are required at Chuquicamata

the earth is several kilometres wide and nearly 1,000m (3,281ft) deep. Enormous trucks the size of houses with tyres 4m (13ft) high remove tonnes of rock each day. More than 600,000 tonnes (590,550 tons) of copper are extracted from the mine every year and the reserve is thought to hold more than 20 per cent of the world's supply. After its first commercial exploitation in 1911, the mine was taken over by the US Anaconda Mining company who developed the town and the mine's infrastructure. The mine was eventually nationalised by the state. The town of Chuquicamata was abandoned in 2006 due to environmental concerns and its citizens relocated to Calama.

Chuquicamata is 18km (11 miles) north of Calama, reached by bus or tour from Calama. You can arrange tours through CODELCO (Tel: 55-327-469. visitas@codelco.cl) or through the tourist office in Calama (Latorre 1689, Tel: 55-345-345).

THE ECONOMY

The strong Chilean economy was a long time in the making and a series of developments since colonisation has led to where it stands today, the third largest in South America. There is a huge trade surplus and foreign debt is quickly disappearing due to the rapidly growing economy. Little of the money trickles down to the lowest levels, however; unemployment remains high and nearly 10 per cent live in poverty.

The first break came from the 1848 California Gold rush, where ships rounding Cabo Horn would stop at several Chilean ports to stock up on grain and other supplies, including Pisco (white grape brandy).

The lands inherited during the War of the Pacific (1879–84) have powered the bulk of Chile's economy since that time. Significant nitrate deposits were a major driving force for many years, until the discovery of synthetic nitrates during World War I. Massive copper reserves were discovered which now account for more than 40 per cent of all exports.

Agriculture is important as well. The wine industry accounts for almost 7 per cent of the world's total export, while salmon farming is a fast-growing industry in the Lakes District and Chiloé, with Chile expected to become the world leader in the next few years.

SAN PEDRO DE ATACAMA AND ENVIRONS
Chug Chug

These 300 or so geoglyphs dot an isolated hillside, comprising geometric shapes, fish, what appears to be a surfer, and sea lions. They are thought to date back to the Incas, the Tihuanacu and regional indigenous groups from the 6th century.

The geoglyphs are located 35km (22 miles) west of Chuquicamata.

Reserva Nacional Los Flamencos

This large reserve encompasses 74,000ha (182,851 acres) of the most interesting attractions around San Pedro de Atacama. High-altitude lakes, unusual geologic formations and a wide variety of wildlife can all be accessed by a good network of roads.

Valle de la Luna

The valley of the moon is known for the surreal landscape of volcanoes, sand dunes and strange rock formations that were created by wind and blown sand. It's most often visited in tours that leave San Pedro de Atacama in the afternoon so you can experience the valley at sunset, when the landscape seems as if it is being painted in gold and shades of red.

The valley is 12km (7½ miles) southwest of San Pedro de Atacama by bus or mountain bike. Tel: 55-851-574. Open: during daylight hours. Admission charge.

San Pedro de Atacama

Far more Indian than the typical Chilean city with *adobe* (mud) houses and locals that still farm in *ayllús* (farming community), the 2,440m

El Tatio geysers

Iglesia San Pedro in San Pedro de Atacama

(8,005ft) San Pedro de Atacama is the gringo hangout of northern Chile, with countless tour offices, restaurants, bars, galleries and gift shops lining the dusty streets. The town was a major stop on pre-Colombian trading routes and later on cattle drives from Argentina to nitrate and mining towns in the Atacama. The small *adobe* church on the Plaza de Armas, Iglesia San Pedro, is the most interesting sight within the village. The 17th-century church is painted white and built with a ceiling constructed of cactus wood and algarrobo with leather fastenings.
San Pedro de Atacama is located one hour southeast of Calama by bus.

Museo Gustavo Le Paige

This museum houses the wonderful findings of Belgian Jesuit priest and archaeologist Gustavo Le Paige, who arrived in Chile in 1953 and spent three decades in this area. There are hundreds of thousands of artefacts including Atacameño ceramics and gold pieces, Incan ceramics, textiles and several mummies and purposely disfigured skulls.
Located beside the Paseo Artesanal north of the Plaza de Armas. Tel: 55-851-002. Open: Mon–Fri 9am–noon & 2–6pm, Sat–Sun 10am–noon & 2–6pm. Admission charge.

El Tatio geysers

El Tatio sits at 4,300m (14,108ft) above sea level, making it one of the world's highest geyser fields. The surreal sights of the 64 sweltering geysers, spurting and steaming, are best seen between 5.30 and 7.00am, before the sun dissolves the vapour. The geothermal field is fed by surrounding volcanoes, and a number of thermal pools can be used for bathing.
The geysers are located 95km (59 miles) north of San Pedro de Atacama. Admission charge.

Salt formations in the Salar de Atacama

ANTOFAGASTA AND ENVIRONS
Antofagasta

Chile's second largest city with a population of more than 300,000, Antofagasta is defined by the bustling port area that once belonged to Bolivia, until the War of the Pacific, and was their major point of export. Today it handles much of the output of the Atacama mines, including Chuquicamata. From the sea lion populated piers near the fish market to the Victorian buildings in the *Barrio Histórico*, the city retains a historic charm lost in the more cosmopolitan ports.

Located 1,361km (846 miles) northwest of Santiago, reached by air or bus.

Bahía Inglesa

This former pirate hangout sits beside beautiful crystal clear waters and beaches made of white seashells. A few trendy restaurants and boutique hotels have sprung up in recent years; however, with just a few apartment blocks and houses, the resort feels completely isolated from any significant population.

Bahía Inglesa is located 6km (4 miles) south of Caldera and 70km (44 miles) northwest of Copiapo.

Laguna Chaxa

This beautiful lake is a part of the larger Salar de Atacama, the largest salt flats in the country at 3,000sq km (1,864sq miles). Other than the strange salt crystallisations found in the lake, it also contains 40 per cent of the world's lithium reserves and is a breeding ground for three species of flamingo (James, Chilean and

Flower in the Atacama Desert

Andean). Several other salt flats, such as the Salar de Tara, are found in the reserve as well.

The lake is located 65km (40 miles) southeast of San Pedro de Atacama. Admission charge.

Parque Nacional Pan de Azúcar

Pan de Azúcar National Park comprises more than 43,000ha (106,252 acres) of coastal desert, sandy beaches and rocky coves. There are more than 100 species of endemic plants and 26 species of cactus, as well as guanaco, sea otters, foxes, sea lions, Humboldt penguins, oyster catchers and the rare Peruvian diving petrel. Campsites are plentiful and you can get local fishermen to take you just offshore to a small island, Pan de Azúcar, inhabited by several thousand penguins and sea lions.

The national park is located 30km (19 miles) north of Chañaral. Admission charge.

Reserva Nacional Pingüino de Humboldt

A rocky shoreline and several small islands just offshore make up this beautiful national reserve in an isolated area between regions III and IV. Bottlenose dolphins and sea otters play in the waters, but the main reason visitors come is for the colonies of sea lions and Humboldt penguins, numbering in the thousands.

No public transport comes to the reserve, but tours from Copiapó come frequently. Admission charge.

LA SERENA
La Serena

One of Chile's best beach resorts, La Serena attracts holidaymakers from across the country during the summer months. They come to soak up the rays or windsurf at a number of white sandy beaches. Economically it is significant as well. Considering that the Norte Chico had such significant deposits of silver and copper, the city was allowed to have its own mint. Although it seems relatively modern from the PanAmericana (PanAmerican Highway), it is the second oldest city in the country, having been founded by Pedro de Valdivia in 1543, as a sea route between Santiago and Lima. The colonial centre is relatively well preserved and the city has nearly 30 churches, most of them built of stone in La Serena's own neo-classical style. The city is overlooked by the Cruz de Tercer Milenio, a 93m (305ft) concrete cross, which was erected atop a hillside in nearby Coquimbo in honour of the late Pope John Paul II.

480km (298 miles) north of Santiago.

Restored colonial buildings on La Serena's Plaza de Armas

Norte Grande and Norte Chico

Pisco distillation process at Pisco Capel

PISCO

Although the World Intellectual Property Organization (WIPO) gave the rights of the name Pisco to Peru in 2005, you wouldn't be able to tell by the consumption in Chile. The country is both the world's largest exporter and consumer of the white grape brandy. Peru may have superior quality, but the Pisco culture in Chile tends to be more commercialised and widespread. The drink was popular in California during the 1848 gold rush, as most of the passenger boats en route to the western United States rounded Cabo Horn and stopped at several Chilean ports.

The spirit is made using fermented white muscatel grapes with a high sugar content that have been planted in northern Chile's arid soil, particularly in the Elqui Valley. The spirit is aged in wooden casks for a period of four to six months. Bottles are labelled by the degree of alcoholic content.

The Pisco Sour is the national cocktail (as well as in Peru) and made from a mixture of lime juice, Pisco and simple syrup. Variations exist that replace the lime with mango, strawberry or other fruits. Other Pisco cocktails include the Chilcano (ginger ale, Pisco and vermouth), the Piscola (Pisco and cola) and the Pisco Martini.

Museo Arqueológico

The main reason to visit this museum is to see the authentic *moai* (heads) from Easter Island. Plaques on the walls tell the story of how the *moai* have been shipped around the world on tours to different museums, and detail the actual shipping process. The museum also has several Atacama mummies and a Diaguita canoe made of sea lion hide, as well as the usual ceramics, weavings and silver pieces.

On the corner of Cordovez and Cienfuegos, three blocks east of the Plaza de Armas. Open: Tue–Fri 9.30am–5.30pm, Sat 10am–1pm & 4–7pm, Sun 10am–1pm. Admission charge.

Muscatel grapes used for Pisco

Stargazing in Atacama

With clear skies nearly every day of the year the Atacama Desert is one of the premier places on earth to scan the night skies, which are the clearest in the southern hemisphere. Multinational organisations have built the majority of the world's greatest astronomical observatories on the tops of many of the mountains. The southern hemisphere offers new opportunities for stargazers, as numerous constellations, such as the Southern Cross or Cruz del Sur, as well as the Clouds of Magellan, can only be seen from here.

Observatory in the Atacama Desert

Increased light pollution from the growing cities nearby and global warming (or quite possibly El Niño effects) has caused the region to have fewer clear nights than just a few decades ago. However, construction of new telescopes is ongoing and doesn't seem to be stopping any time soon.

The **European Southern Observatory** (*120km/75 miles south of Antofagasta. Tel: 55-260-032. www.eso.org*) was built with the help of eight European nations. It has built the Paranal Observatory, which consists of four 8.2m (27ft) telescopes, creating one Very Large Telescope (VLT). At this time, it is the most powerful optical telescope in the world. Visits are allowed during the day in the last two weekends of every month, with the exception of December. The same organisation also maintains La Silla Observatory further north.

The **Cerro Tololo Inter-American Observatory** (*70km/44 miles east of La Serena. Tel: 51-205-200. www.ctio.noao.edu*), meanwhile, owns a 4m (13ft) Blanco telescope on Cerro Tololo, and its complement, the new 4.1m (13½ft) SOAR Telescope, which is on the adjacent Cerro Pachon. Next to it is the 8m (26ft)

Gemini South infrared telescope. By using infrared technology, astronomers are able to peer through vast clouds of cosmic dust that usually obscure star birth to view the cores of distant galaxies. There are a number of smaller telescopes there as well. Two free tours of the facility are offered on Saturdays, at 9am and 1pm.

Las Campanas Observatory (*157km/98 miles north of La Serena. Tel: 51-207-301. www.lco.cl*), owned by the Carnegie Institution of Washington, owns two 6.5m (21ft) telescopes, but it is the Giant Magellan Telescope that is gathering the most attention. This is the product of more than a century of research, and it is thought it will open a new window to the universe, with a resolving power of a 24.5m

(80ft) primary mirror, which is quite a bit larger than any other telescope ever built. It won't be completed until 2016.

ALMA (Atacama Very Large Telescope), which won't be finished until 2011, consists of 64 12m (39ft) antennae, making it the largest radio telescope in the world. It will be able to 'listen' to objects in space 100 times more magnified than ever before. It will be located 40km (25 miles) east of San Pedro de Atacama.

Sadly, the observatories only allow daytime visits. If you intend to come here to actually use a telescope, visit the much smaller **Observatorio Comunal Cerro Mamalluca** community observatory (*see p61*) near Vicuña, which is open to the public during the night and offers guided tours and lectures.

Visit the Cerro Mamalluca Observatory and have a look through their telescope

Excursion: Elqui Valley

The centre of Chile's Pisco production, ostrich farms and a new age spiritual centre, the Elqui Valley is thought to be magical. Pilgrims come and go, living in esoteric communities, practising meditation, Tibetan Buddhism, or a number of guru-led sects. The mountain scenery combined with the fertile valley is spectacular and the clear skies have led to a number of observatories being built on the top of almost every mountain.

1 Vicuña

The small town of Vicuña is the centre of excursions in the valley and has a good tourist infrastructure, with banks, restaurants and hotels around its charming plaza. The town was the birthplace of Nobel prize-winning poet Gabriela Mistral (1889–1957). **The Gabriela Mistral Museum** documents her life in the town and her literary career, comprising manuscripts, books, photographs, letters and personal

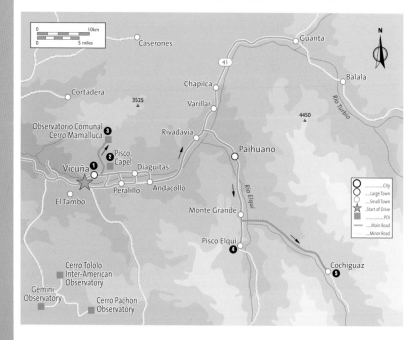

objects. Mistral's tomb can be visited in **Monte Grande**, southeast of Vicuña. (*Calle Gabriela Mistral 759. Tel: 51-411-223. Open: Mon–Fri 10am–1pm & 2.30–5.45pm, Sat 10am–1pm & 3–5.45pm, Sun 10am–1pm).*
Admission charge.
Drive for 20 minutes northeast to reach Pisco Capel.
Vicuña is 62km (39 miles) east of La Serena. Tourist Office: on the Plaza de Armas in Vicuña. Tel: 51-209-125.

2 Pisco Capel

This Pisco producer seems to be winning the advertising war and its factory and vineyards are the most visited, the largest and most commercial. Twenty-minute tours of the plant are followed by small samples and sales. The plant also produces the famed *pajarete* dessert wine.
Tel: 51-411-251. www.piscocapel.com. Open: Jan–Feb 10am–6pm, Mar–Dec 10am–12.30pm & 2.30–6pm.
Drive north for a few more kilometres to the Observatorio.

3 Observatorio Comunal Cerro Mamalluca

A community nighttime observatory built specifically for tourists, there are a number of telescopes, the largest magnification possible being 140 times, which is enough for good views of star clusters, galaxies, planets and of course the moon. Tours of the facility lasts several hours and are combined with lectures and guided explanations.

Office in Vicuña at Av Gabriela Mistral 260. Tel: 51-411-352.
www.mamalluca.org.
Return towards Vicuña and turn left on route 41. After Rivadavia, turn right for Pisco Elqui (37km (23 miles) southeast of Vicuña).

4 Tres Erres Pisco plantation, Pisco Elqui

This brand is far better than Capel and a major Pisco label. Free 30-minute tours are followed by free samples of the premium brand. The town was renamed Pisco Elqui in the 1930s to help promote its number one product and hurt Peru's claims to the white grape brandy.
Tel: 51-451-358. Open: 11am–7pm.
Turn back towards Monte Grande and turn right for Cochiguaz, 37km (23 miles) southeast.

5 Cochiguaz

UFO sightings are frequent here, in what some suggest is a nucleus of cosmic energy. A few countryside resorts have sprung up, most with solar power and offering new age treatments.

Sky and desert in the Elqui Valley

Central Chile

Often overshadowed by the vibrant capital, the region surrounding Santiago is filled with some of the country's top attractions. The best vineyards lie here in the sunny valleys, as well as many of the best ski resorts, which sit amid the foothills of the Andes. Beach resorts line the coast and pair with Valparaíso, the country's most romantic and unusual city and a photographer's dream come true.

The coast is home to the large, vibrant and historically important cities of Valparaíso and Viña del Mar, which are two favourite stops for travellers and the highlight of many people's itineraries. Vineyards can be found in nearly every valley. The Casablanca Valley between Santiago and Valparaíso is best for white wines, while the Maule and Colchagua valleys to the south are world renowned for their reds, such as Cabernet Sauvignon, Carmenère and Merlot.

With Santiago in the centre, getting around the region is relatively easy as connections from the capital by bus or train can be made to anywhere.

Cabernet Sauvignon grapes flourish in the Mediterranean climes of central Chile

The Ascensor Artillería is a working national monument

VALPARAÍSO AND ENVIRONS
Valparaíso

Chileans always saw Valpo, as it is known, as a bit more 'rough and tumble' than Santiago, but in 2003 it was declared a UNESCO World Heritage Site, and everyone has begun to take notice.

The port city is one of the most dreamy and unusual cities in the world. Houses share steep hillsides with funicular railways. Classical music fills the air in a maze of narrow, cobblestone streets. Romantic cafés dangle on terraces overlooking the city and the Pacific.

Lying 120km (74 1/2 miles) northwest of Santiago, Valparaíso, nicknamed *La Perla del Pacífico* (the Pearl of the Pacific), is Chile's principal port and second largest city. Wedged between steep hills and the Pacific on a slender strip of land, it has character and atmosphere, and a history to reflect that. In its early days it was sacked numerous times by pirates, and by Sir Francis Drake in 1577. It saw booms from nitrate and the California gold rush, but fell upon hard times after a detrimental earthquake in 1906 that measured 8.6 on the Richter scale, and then the building of the Panama Canal in 1914, which took much of the traffic away. Many locals turned to petty crime and drink. In the early 20th century it was said to have more than 1,500 bars, in other words, one for every 35 adult men. The National Congress, built in 1990 on the orders of General Pinochet, did little to help the economy of the region.

New life

The recovery came from the most unlikely of places. After warnings of the city heading to ruin and the Ascensores being listed as one of the world's most threatened monuments in 1996, a rediscovery of the city's heritage occurred and what began as an outcry from artists and bohemians quickly became a major community development. Hence, Valpo has had a facelift in the last few years. Art galleries, craft shops, trendy cafés and restaurants pepper once empty streets. The Muelle Prat pier was recently redeveloped and is now a lively market area. More than 40 cruise ships dock at the port from October to April, bringing more than 80,000 tourists. Life has been pumped back into the city.

Then again, some things in Valpo are just as they always were. A weekend antique market lines the streets around Plaza O'Higgins. At the town's famous Cinzano bar, singers and crooners still jam the bar until the wee hours with light-footed couples. The ascensor lifts have been restored and still move passengers up and down the hillsides. They have now been named a National Monument.

Ascensores

The rickety ascensores are the defining characteristic of Valparaíso and riding them is the one activity that no visitor should miss. They have been restored since they were listed as 'endangered' by the World Monuments Fund in 1996, and are as fashionable as ever. There are 15 funiculars set on the hills around Valparaíso, running on train tracks with cables linking an upward-bound car to a downward-bound car. The cables pass through a large pulley at the top, so each car counterweights the other. The ride up or down usually takes about one or two minutes. Here are some of the most notable ascensores:

Ascensor Artillería (*Open: 7am–11.30pm*), near the port, has sweeping views of the entire city and the bay. It was originally used to transport cadets to the naval school (now a naval museum) that once stood on top of the hill.

Ascensor Concepción (*Open: 7am–8.30pm*), built in 1883, begins across from the Reloj Turri clocktower, and was originally steam powered. It leads to one of the most charming neighbourhoods in the city, with narrow winding streets full of colourful houses.

Ascensor Espíritu Santo (*Open: 7am–11pm*) near Plaza Victoria, leads not only to Neruda's Valparaíso home but to an open-air art gallery with more than 20 murals on Cerro Bellavista.

Ascensor Polanco (*Open: 7am–11pm*) is actually a lift, starting underground (it is reached by a tunnel) and ending at the top of a tower, 30.5m (100ft) or so above

ground at the top of Cerro Polanco.

Ascensor Reina Victoria (*Open: 7am–11pm*) takes you to a former prison that has been transformed into a cultural centre and park, as well as the oldest building in the city, a gunpowder storehouse. Concerts and plays are frequently held on the site.

Rides cost 100–200 pesos each way, depending on the ascensor.

Congreso Nacional

This colossal structure was a $100 million investment by Pinochet in the place of one of his boyhood homes. The modern, cement structure, completed in 1990, seems relatively out of place in retro Valpo, and many wish the Congress would move back to Santiago with the executive branch.

Opposite the bus terminal.

Iglesia La Matriz

Originally built in 1559, this church was razed on several occasions due to pirate attacks and earthquakes. The present construction dates to 1842, although earthquakes have made restorations essential over the years, including the lowering of the tower, which was originally 25m (82ft) high.

Just uphill from the Mercado Central.

La Sebastiana

Pablo Neruda's Valparaíso home extends over four floors and is much like his other homes in Santiago and Isla Negra. It has his strange collections of art, peculiar objects and stained-glass windows and is where Neruda watched the New Year's Eve fireworks display over the bay from his lookout every year. The Fundación Neruda has built a small art gallery and café at the side of the house.

The museum can be reached via Ascensor Espíritu Santo.
Tel: 32-256-606. Open: Tue–Sun 10.30am–2.30pm & 3.30–6pm.
Admission charge.
Valparaíso is located 1½ hours west of Santiago by bus.

The Congreso Nacional was moved to Valparaíso in General Pinochet's era

VIÑA DEL MAR

Not as compelling as Valparaíso just 10km (6 miles) down the coast, but visited far more often by Santiaguinos who appreciate the commercial appeal. Viña is one of the most popular beach resorts in the country and is lined with high-rise apartments, casinos, chain restaurants and shopping centres. It manages to retain quite a bit of charm, however, as there are a number of turn-of-the-20th-century mansions, castles and beautiful parks. Riding in a horse-drawn carriage is still a popular pastime to this day. It is known as the Garden City because of the palm and banana

Playa Acapulco is a busy beach near the centre

trees that line its streets. The city plays host to an international music festival for five days at the end of February each year, which features artists and performers from around the world and attracts more than a million people to the region.

Beaches

Although the city has quite a bit of historical and cultural significance, it is the beaches that attract the most visitors. During the summer months the white sandy stretches of sand are filled with everything from sun worshippers and umbrellas to candyfloss vendors, volleyball nets and sea lions. An activity-laden boardwalk runs parallel to the beaches, which extend far north of the city to the apartment-filled suburbs of Reñaca and Concón.

Buses and taxis run to, from and along Av Peru, which hugs the coastline.

Jardín Botánico Nacional

Chile's national botanical garden comprises 61ha (151 acres) of native and exotic plants such as cacti and palms, as well as many species from Easter Island, including the endangered Toromino tree. The park was designed by a French landscape artist to house the plants collected by Croatian-born nitrate magnate Pascual Baburizza during his world travels.

Twenty minutes southeast of downtown by bus or taxi. Open: 10am–6.30pm. Admission charge.

Luxury condominiums line the coast at Playa El Sol as thousands of sunbathers crowd the beaches below

Museo Palacio Rioja

Although the façade of this mansion is French neo-classical, the inside is a *mélange* of European styles from baroque to French Empire. The inside now houses a municipal museum and frequently holds concerts and screenings.

Located in the Quinta Rioja, at Quillota 214. Open: Tue–Sun 10am–1.30pm & 3–5.30pm. Admission charge.

Parque Quinta Vergara

These beautifully maintained gardens were once part of the estate belonging to the wealthy Alvares-Vergara family, who engineered the railway from Santiago to the coast, and developed much of the city. Many of the plants were brought back from the family's travels to Asia and Australia. Their mansion, the stunning Venetian style **Palacio Vergara**, is home of the Museo Municipal de Bellas Artes, one of the most significant European and national art collections in the country. The park is also home to an amphitheatre, which holds the International Music Festival each year.

Open: Tue–Sun 10am–1.30pm & 3–5.30pm. Admission charge.
Viña del Mar is located ten minutes north of Valparaíso, reachable by bus or tram that runs between the cities.

ISLA NEGRA AND TALCA
Isla Negra

Isla Negra is not actually an island at all, but rather a point. Pablo Neruda nicknamed it after the black island of Sumatra, which he had visited. Neruda's favourite, and most often visited, home is here and was once owned by a Spanish captain. Much of the house was built in the 1940s by the poet and Catalan architect Germán Rodriguez Arias. It was raided just three days after the 1973 coup, while Neruda was dying of cancer in Santiago.

Part of the roof was designed to reflect the houses of Temuco, where Neruda grew up listening to the rain on the roof. Other items, such as the collections of masks, shells, minerals, miniature sailing boats, carved wooden statues and insects reflect the poet's travels and literary life. (Note the fireplace adorned with lapis lazuli.) The tomb of Neruda and his third wife Matilda overlooks the sea, towards the point where he dictated his poem 'Disposiciones' from *Canto General*:

'Comrades, bury me in Isla Negra
in front of the sea I know,
of every shore rugged with stones
and with waves my lost eyes
will not see again…'

Bus from either Santiago (1³/4 hrs) or Valparaíso (1¹/2 hrs). Museum Poeta Neruda. Tel: (56) 35-461-284. www.fundacionneruda.org. Open: Tue–Sun 10am–8pm. Admission charge.

Rocky, inspiring coast at Isla Negra

Talca

The centre of the wine-growing industry of the Maule Valley, Talca has a climate perfect for growing wine and a pleasant climate for those looking to escape the smog of Santiago for a few days. The town is of historical significance as well. A colonial house just off the recently restored Plaza de Armas is where Bernardo O'Higgins signed Chile's 1818 Declaration of Independence.

Talca is 257km (160 miles) south of Santiago, three hours by bus or train.

Pablo Neruda's house, his favourite and most eccentric, on Isla Negra

Central Chile

Chilean wine

Chilean wine is well known on the international market and is constantly battling with Argentina to be the premier wine-producing country in South America. Natural borders protect the wine-growing regions: the Atacama Desert to the north, the Andes to the east, the Pacific to the west and the Antarctic to the south. These are the only vineyards in the world to be free of mildew and phylloxera.

The Spanish brought winemaking to Chile as early as the middle of the 16th century, although it wasn't until the latter half of the 19th century with the arrival of a number of French winemakers that the industry started to produce premium wines. Between 1995 and 2005 the total area of all vineyards expanded by an astounding 80 per cent and the country now produces 5 per cent of the world's annual harvest, with more than two thirds being exported.

A number of reds are Chile's highlights; however, one grape has come to the attention of the international community more than any other. Originally from the Bordeaux region of France, the Carmenère grape has come into its

Over 60 per cent of Chile's total annual wine production is exported

own in Chile and has fared far better than it ever did in Europe. The grape, which had been misidentified in Chile as a Merlot for many years, was thought to have been lost to phylloxera, which struck vineyards around the world in the latter half of the 19th century. On further inspection in 1994, and to the astonishment of the wine world, oenologists discovered that many of Chile's Merlots were actually true Carmenère. Along with Cabernet Sauvignon, it is the most planted grape in the country.

Valle de Casablanca (Casablanca Valley)

Between Santiago and Valparaíso, this coastal valley (*www.casablancavalley.cl*) has temperatures that do not reach above 20°C (68°F) during the vines' vegetative period, which creates excellent conditions for a number of white varietals such as Chardonnay and Sauvignon Blanc, as well as Pinot Noir.

Valle de Colchagua (Colchagua Valley)

In the Rancagua region, 152km (95 miles) south of Santiago near the town of Santa Cruz, the Colchagua Valley (*www.colchaguavalley.cl*) is one of the country's most prestigious wine-growing regions and the first established and most expensive wine route, with many resort-style hotels, immaculate tasting rooms and superb facilities. Many of the best wines in the country come from here, including Cabernet Sauvignon, Merlot, Carmenère and Chardonnay.

Valle del Maipo (Maipo Valley)

Some of the biggest names in Chilean wine can be found near Santiago, in what is called the Maipo Valley (*www.valledelmaipo.com*) where the most visited wineries in the country lie. Concha y Toro, the country's most world-renowned name, has a large

Viña Concha y Toro vineyards grow Cabernet Sauvignon grapes

property near the town of Pirque where the Concha y Toro, Don Melchor and Casillero del Diabolo labels were created. Viña Cousiño Macul, another of Chile's top names can be found here, actually within the city limits. They produce a range of good reds (*see pp36–7*).

Valle del Maule (Maule Valley)

The Maule Valley has the most cellars in the country and a well-organised wine route (*www.valledelmaule.cl*). The Mediterranean climate found between the foothills of the Andes and the Chilean plain around Talca is perfect for producing Cabernet Sauvignon, Carmenère and Merlot.

Drive: Ruta del Vino Maule Valley

The Ruta del Vino, or wine route, is a common feature in Chile's wine-growing regions. The route in the Maule Valley, near Talca, is one of the most visited. The valley boasts the largest number of wine cellars in the country and has more than 25,000ha (61,774 acres) of vineyards. The Mediterranean-like weather makes it a pleasant weekend retreat. Cabernet Sauvignon, Merlot, Carmenère and Chardonnay are all grown here in a range of vineyards, from rustic to contemporary.

1 Tours can be arranged from the Ruta del Vino Office, Villa Cultural Huilquilemu (*Tel: 71-246-460. www.valledelmaule.cl*), on the road to San Clemente, ten minutes from Talca. You can use their transport or your own and can include two or three vineyards of your choice. You can either contact the office first or contact the vineyards directly but you should not just turn up at a vineyard.

Drive 7km (4¹/4 miles) northeast to Viña Calina.

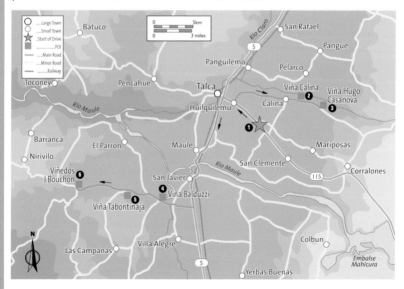

2 Viña Calina

These sprawling vineyards sit on an 85ha (210-acre) site and are one of the most modern facilities in the country. The vineyard was established in 1993 and exports throughout the world.
Tel: 71-263-126. www.calina.cl.
Drive 1km (²/₃ mile) east to Viña Hugo Casanova.

3 Viña Hugo Casanova

This is a small, rustic vineyard surrounding a colonial hacienda. Northern Italian immigrants, the Casanovas arrived in the 19th century. The vineyard produces 1.3 million litres (almost 300,000 gallons) annually which is exported around the world under a number of names. The tours are brief but friendly, and guides are knowledgeable.
Tel: 71-246-460. www.hugocasanova.cl.
Drive back to Huilquilemu and turn right then left on route 5; pass San Javier and turn right to Viña Balduzzi.

4 Viña Balduzzi

Viña Balduzzi is set in a 100-year-old cluster of colonial buildings and manicured gardens. The 30-minute tours describe the entire wine-making process from grape to bottle, and leave you with a taste of four wines.
Tel: 73-322-138. www.balduzziwines.cl.
Drive a little further west to Viña Tabontinaja.

5 Viña Tabontinaja

More of a luxury wine resort with a spa that includes wine therapy, these are the vineyards of Gillmore wines, started in 1993. Set on beautiful land surrounding a small village, this is one of the original *agroturismo* resorts in the country and the owners encourage visitors to get to know the wine-making process.
Tel: 73-197-5539. www.gillmore.cl.
Drive a few kilometres west of Tabontinaja.

6 Viñedos J Bouchon

This vineyard was established by a French immigrant from Bordeaux in 1892 and encompasses approximately 370ha (914 acres) of mostly 60-year-old vines producing Cabernet Sauvignon, Merlot, Malbec, Carmenère, Syrah, Sauvignon Blanc and Chardonnay.
Tel: 73-246-9778. www.jbouchon.cl

Viña Calina vineyards

Lakes District

The land is some of the most scenic in the southern hemisphere, with emerald lakes, fresh air, temperate forests and some of the most spectacular mountains and snow-capped volcanoes in the Andes. Some of the most visited national parks in the country are found here, and adventure sports abound from skiing to climbing, and from hiking to rafting. First-class resorts and casinos are set beside fern-covered hot springs and black sand beaches that adorn the lakes.

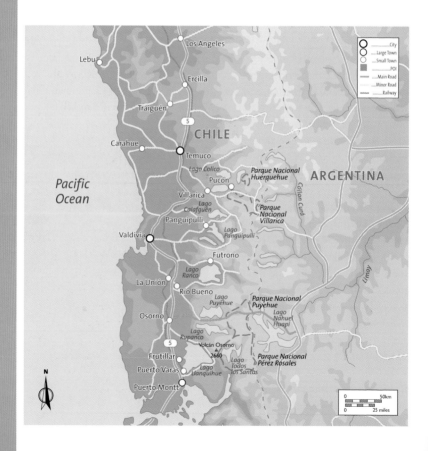

Lago Llanquihue with Volcán Osorno in the background

This was the heartland of the Mapuche people who, for centuries, were able to keep the Spanish at bay. It wasn't until the mid-19th century, when the Chilean army, equipped with modern weaponry, was able to establish themselves in the region. Today, as property prices are constantly rising because of wealthy Santiaguinos buying country homes, the Mapuche are being pushed further into the fringes of the region. From the 1850s to the 1870s the Chilean government, in an effort to colonise the area and Europeanise the country, invited Germans from the Black Forest to populate the region. There was a labour crisis in Germany at the time and the land was covered with lakes, mountains and forests, not entirely different from their own. Their influence can be seen today in the architecture, the farming, the food and even the beer.

PUERTO MONTT

The commercial and transport centre of Southern Chile is set among fertile green hills and small islets. On clear days you can see snow-capped volcanoes on the horizon.

Being the centre of the salmon industry has made Puerto Montt the fastest growing city in Southern Chile, with approximately 170,000 residents. Though much of the city is contemporary, there are a few districts that were unscathed or quickly rebuilt after the 1960 earthquake and these retain a certain charm reminiscent of other Lakes District towns, or even nearby Chiloé. The quaint fishing village and ferry port of Angelmó has a laid-back atmosphere and characterful red, yellow and blue tin-roofed houses. On the southwestern edge of town, lining the seafront avenue, rows of stalls sell smoked mussels, edible sea plants, crafts, woodcarvings and antiques. The road culminates in a bustling produce and fish market, lined with seafood restaurants. The main port to the east has been redesigned to accept major cruise ships that dock daily here during the summer.

A wide variety of shellfish is available here

Casa del Arte Diego Rivera

This art gallery and cultural centre was donated by the Mexican government shortly after the 1960 earthquake. The art of local and international artists is displayed on the top floor, while the ground floor holds theatre, dance and film exhibitions.

One block east of the Plaza Quillota 116. Open: Mon–Fri 10am–1pm & 3–9pm, Sat–Sun 10am–6pm. Free admission.

Catedral

Made of the local alerce tree, this neo-classical cathedral, built in 1856, is the oldest building left standing in the city after the 1960 earthquake.

The Plaza de Armas, just off the pier. Opening hours vary.

Museo Juan Pablo II

This excellent and modern museum is dedicated to the late Pope John Paul II in honour of his 1987 visit. The rooms display the natural and human history of the area, with one of the best collections of artefacts from southern Chile. Detailed maps and photographs show the transformation of the city as it has grown.

The waterfront beside the bus terminal. Av Diego Portales 991. Open: Mon–Fri 9am–7pm, Sat–Sun 10am–6pm. Admission charge.

Puerto Montt is the transport hub of southern Chile. Connections by plane, ferry and bus can be made to anywhere in the country. The city is located 1,020km (634 miles) south of Santiago on the PanAmerican Highway.

Piercings and handicrafts for sale at Puerto Montt's waterfront

ATTRACTIONS IN THE LAKES DISTRICT
Cruce de Lagos

The *Cruce de Lagos*, or Crossing of the Lakes, is a popular, if pricey, journey on a combination of buses and luxury catamarans to Bariloche, Argentina. For more information visit the website of the transport company that organises the trip: *www.crucedelagos.cl*.

You can begin the journey as early as Puerto Montt; however, most book tickets from Puerto Varas. Departures leave daily from September to March, and weekdays during the rest of the year.

Frutillar

Just north of Puerto Varas, on the coast of Lago Llanquihue, is this charming lakeside retreat where the German

The snow-covered volcano rising above Puerto Montt and its harbour

influence is overwhelming at times. Each February the town hosts Semanas Musicales, one of the most important classical music festivals in Chile. *Frutillar is 40 minutes north of Puerto Varas by bus.*

Parque Nacional Pérez Rosales

Founded in 1926, Parque Nacional Pérez Rosales is the oldest national park in Chile. More than 120,000 visitors make their way annually to the 250,000ha (617,742-acre) park to see its abundance of flora and fauna. Three stunning volcanoes, Osorno, Puntiagudo and Tronador serve as the backdrop of the park's centrepiece, Lago Todos los Santos. A well-trodden hiking trail from the lake leads to the second most notable attraction, the Saltos de Petrohué, where the Persian-green water shoots through a lava tunnel created by the 1950 eruption of Osorno. A perfect photo opportunity awaits you.

Daily buses from Ensenada, Puerto Varas and Puerto Montt.
Tel: 65-486-115. Open: daily Dec–Feb 8.30am–8pm, Mar–Nov 8.30am–6.30pm. Admission charge. For more information contact the CONAF information centre in the park.

Parque Nacional Puyehue

In the 1960 eruption of Volcán Puyehue, the top blew, covering a large tract of wilderness with lava, altering the landscape dramatically. The result is a 107,000ha (264,393-acre) mix of contrasting landscape of trees, waterfalls, dunes, hot springs, mountains and lakes. The dense evergreen forests are home to towering Ulmo trees, puma, pudú (a rare deer) and numerous bird species.

The southwest slope of Volcán Casablanca becomes a popular ski resort during the winter months of June to October.

The park is located 75km (47 miles) east of Osorno via route 215, which continues to the Argentine border.
The CONAF information centre is located at the hot springs.
Open: Dec–Feb 9am–7pm, Mar–Nov 9am–1pm & 2–8.30pm.
Admission charge.

Puerto Varas

In a beautiful setting on Lago Llanquihue, with views of the Osorno and Calbuco volcanoes, is this small town that became a full-scale resort. It is considered a less crowded alternative to Pucón, with a burgeoning infrastructure where any number of adventure activities and excursions into national parks can be made. In winter, the only visitors are skiers who come for nearby Volcán Osorno. The town displays classic German architecture from the early 20th century, particularly the Iglesia del Sagrado Corazón, which was based on the Marienkirche church in Nagold, Germany.

Puerto Varas is 30 minutes north of Puerto Montt by bus.

Chile's ski resorts

During the construction of a railway from Santiago to Mendoza in Argentina, English engineers working on the site began to ski down the slopes in order to get to lower altitudes. When the railway was complete, they began taking the train to get to the tops of the mountains just to ski down it again. Thus began the Chilean ski industry. Unlike those in Argentina, most of the Chilean resorts are for the country's élite as well as international visitors. They are posh and expensive, surrounded by luxury lodges and geared towards week-long stays. Many international ski teams reside here for training

during the winter months of June to October, while it is summer in the northern hemisphere. Most of the areas sit above 3,300m (10,827ft), with long treeless runs, covered in deep, dry powder. A number of the runs actually sit on the slopes of volcanoes such as Villarica, near Pucón.

Chapa Verde

Chapa Verde was built for the copper workers, but now is open to the public. There are four lifts and 22 runs of good quality. It lacks many of the crowds and prices that plague some other resorts. *The resort is located 50km (31 miles) northeast of Rancagua. www.chapaverde.cl. Tel: 72-217-651.*

Osorno

This resort near Puerto Varas takes you to the slopes of a perfect conical-shaped volcano. There are just four lifts, which are all quite long and there is a good range of skill levels offered. *Volcán Osorno is reached by shuttle bus from Puerto Varas. For more information visit: www.volcanosorno.com. Tel: 65-233-445.*

The pristine snow at Valle Nevado

Valley between snow-covered mountains

Portillo

Located in the Aconcagua Valley, Portillo is the top ski resort in Chile. It is set on the gorgeous alpine Laguna del Inca on the Argentine border, surrounded by outrageously expensive hotels and restaurants. There is also an alpine village complete with ice skating rink, gym, heated outdoor pool, shopping, spas and a cinema. Many of the world's top skiers use Portillo as their summer base and a number of speed records have been set here. There are 17 powder-filled runs ranging in altitude from 2,600 to 3,300m (8,530 to 10,827ft), many going for several kilometres. The terrain is suitable for all skill levels. *Portillo can be reached by bus from Santiago in three and a half hours. For more information visit: www.skiportillo.com*

Termas de Chillán

This ski and spa resort is one of the best known at international level and the most complete for an all out leisure destination. The 10,000ha (24,710 acres) of terrain has the longest run in South America at 13km (8 miles), 11 lifts and nearly 30 runs. As far as size, this is the largest of Chile's resorts. *Termas de Chillán is located 489km (304 miles) south of Santiago, reachable by bus or by plane from Concepción. For more information visit: www.termaschillan.cl. Tel: 42-434-200.*

Valle Nevado

Due to its proximity to the capital, Valle Nevado attracts élite Santiaguinos and has a haughty atmosphere much like that of Portillo. The 27 runs go as high as 3,700m (12,139ft), the longest 3km (2 miles) in length. There are eight lifts, as well as easy arrangements for heli-skiing. *Valle Nevado is just 60km (37 miles) from Santiago airport. For more information visit: www.vallenevado.com. Tel: 2-477-7700.*

VALDIVIA AND VILLARICA
Valdivia

Valdivia, or *La Perla del Sur* (the Pearl of the South), was the initial centre of German immigration in Chile and they set up some of the country's finest institutions, which has led to a colossal student population today. The city sits amid three rivers, the Calle Calle, Cau Cau and Cruces, where tour boats ply the waters to and from the city to the majestic Spanish forts that dot the banks. At the time of founding in 1552 by Pedro de Valdivia, this was the southernmost Spanish city in the world. In order to protect it from the Mapuche, pirate and later rebel army attacks, the rivers surrounding the city became some of the most heavily fortified in the Americas. At the riverside market, the Feria Fluvial (*Open: 8am–3pm*), overweight sea lions float back and forth in front of the fish market fighting with seabirds for scraps.

Kuntsmann Brewery

Founded by the Kuntsmann family, who arrived from Germany in the 1850s, this brewery quickly grew and today distributes its beers across Chile. The beers produced on the premises include bock, toro bayo, lager, honey-flavoured and even a non-alcoholic variety. Each are made according to the German Edicto de la Pureza de 1516 (German Edict of Purity of 1516). There is a brief guided tour of the brewery and onsite museum for every visitor, followed by samples. A beerfest is held at the end of each January.

The brewery is located on Isla Teja, 3km (2 miles) northwest of the centre, reachable by taxi or any bus heading to Niebla. Open: Nov–Mar daily noon–1am, Apr–Oct Mon–Sat noon–midnight, Sun noon–7pm. Tel: 63-292-969. www.lacerveceria.cl.

Museo Histórico y Arqueológico

This beautiful museum, set in a colonial mansion on the riverfront, houses a number of Mapuche artefacts, as well as a good display on the early German settlers and their daily lives.

The museum sits just across the Río Valdivia from the plaza, on Isla Teja near the Puente (bridge) Pedro de Valdivia on Los Robles. Tel: 63-212-872. Open: Dec–Mar 9am–1pm & 2.30–6pm, Apr–Nov 10am–1pm & 2–6pm. Admission charge.

German architecture in central Valdivia

Feria Fluvial in Valdivia

Spanish forts

A number of 17th-century Spanish forts can be found in the area to the southwest of Valdivia at the confluence of the Ríos Valdivia and Tornagaleones. Built in 1645, Fuerte Niebla, on the north side of the river 18km (11 miles) from the city at the mouth of the Río Valdivia, sits on a high cliff adorned with cannons. Across the river, Castillo de Corral, beside Valdivia's main port, was built in 1645, but reconstructed several times since. Recreations of military drills can be seen during the summer at 4.30pm and 6.15pm. During much of the late 18th century, the population of Valdivia was forced to live at Castillo San Pedro de Alcántara on Isla Mancera, due to Mapuche raids.

The forts can be reached by boat tours from the Feria Fluvial, or by bus from Valdivia. Fuerte Niebla. Open: Nov–Mar Tue–Sun 10am–7pm, Apr–Oct Tue–Sun 10am–5.30pm. Castillo de Corral. Open: Dec–Mar daily 9am–9pm, Apr–Nov daily 10am–7pm. Castillo San Pedro de Alcántara. Open: Dec–Mar daily 10am–2pm & 3–7pm, Apr–Nov Tue–Sun 10am–2pm & 3–7pm.

Valdivia is located 160km (100 miles) southwest of Temuco and 160km (100 miles) north of Puerto Montt, accessed by bus or plane.

Villarica

Founded in 1552, this town and its 800 residents were besieged by the Mapuche in 1599–1602, led by Cacique Cuminaguel, after numerous other uprisings. It wasn't until 1882 that the Mapuche allowed the Chilean state to reestablish the city. The lakeside retreat is more mellow and filled with more character than nearby Pucón.

Villarica is 20 minutes by bus from Pucón.

PUCÓN, TEMUCO AND NATIONAL PARKS
Parque Nacional Huerquehue

Set amid some of the Lakes District's most beautiful scenery, Parque Huerquehue covers 12,500ha (30,887 acres) of araucaria forest, emerald lakes and waterfalls. Good hiking trails crisscross the park, which has a number of great campsites and lodges set beside pristine mountain lakes.

The park, open year round, is reached in one hour by frequent buses from Pucón. Admission charge.

Parque Nacional Villarica

With easy access from Pucón, the more than 60,000ha (148,258 acres) of Parque Nacional Villarica receives one of the highest visitor counts of any national park. The park's highlights are the three volcanoes: Villarica (2,847m/9,340ft), Quetrupillán (2,360m/7,743ft) and Lanín (3,764m/12,349ft). The snow-covered peak Volcán Villarica is one of Chile's most active volcanoes and has destroyed several villages in the area as recently as 1971, when Coñaripe was covered by an avalanche caused by lava melting glacial ice on the mountain. Climbing the volcano is one of the most sought after feats in Chile and can be completed by anyone with the correct equipment. The climb is completed in a day, and helped by a ski lift in one section for an extra few pesos. Skiing is offered down the slopes of the active volcano during winter

Volcán Villarica hovering over Pucón

(see Portillo and ski resorts pp82–3 for more information).
Parque Nacional Villarica is reached by taxi or tour bus in 30 minutes from Pucón.

Pucón

Set between a dazzling mountain lake and a volcano, this resort town has become the centre of Chile's adventure sport industry and home to a plethora of new age shops and spas, trendy bars and restaurants, and boutique hotels. The summer population of tourists fills the town to the brim and the activity options are endless. During the summer, the beautiful black sand beach at Playa Grande, north of the centre, is packed with sun-seekers and vendors offering everything from ice cream and beer, to kayaks and jet skis. At night the volcano emits an eerie red glow over the city. A traffic light-style warning system set up across town shows up-to-the-minute information on the state and safety of the volcano.

Pucón is located three hours southeast of Temuco and 11 hours south of Santiago by bus.

Temuco

A sprawling city of 250,000 residents, it is a commercial and transport hub, where the national poet Pablo Neruda grew up. The city sits in what was once strong Mapuche territory. Although smaller settlements existed before, Mapuche attacks didn't allow a permanent settlement until 1881. Just north of the city is the Cerro Ñielol Natural Monument – a hill with 90ha (222 acres) of forests and home to Chile's national flower, the copihue. A site called La Patagua, is also where the Mapuche surrendered their land to the colonists in 1881. The Mapuche, who now live outside the city, make their way into town to buy and sell their woollen goods, crafts and produce in a number of markets and shops around the town.

Temuco is located 675km (419 miles) south of Santiago, eight hours by bus, nine hours by train.

One of the hiking trails at Parque Nacional Huerquehue

The Mapuche

The Incas never conquered the fierce Mapuche warriors. Neither did the Spanish. The Chilean government only incorporated their lands into the state in the middle of the 19th century. The Mapuche staged a 300-year battle that was the most successful indigenous fight in the Americas – and it is still ongoing against cultural onslaught and expanding cities.

Mapuche woollen goods

Spanish effect

When the Spanish arrived in Chile the indigenous population was similar to what it was today. However, by the end of the 16th century it had dwindled to a few hundred thousand due to European illnesses that swept across the people like wildfire. The Mapuche managed to defend their lands, however, and they quickly destroyed any Spanish settlement south of the Río Biobío. The Mapuche sided with the colonists when they split with Spain. During the Pacification of Araucanía in 1881, however, an increasing colonial presence pushed the Mapuche further and further to the fringes of their own land.

During the Pinochet regime, large pieces of land were taken from the Mapuche and given to forestry companies, who cut down the native forests to plant faster growing eucalyptus and pine. Even after the collapse of the regime, the land was never given back and the destruction of the forest has only increased each year. Although court battles are frequent, the government has sided with big business in most cases.

A Mapuche woman in Temuco

Fightback

The 1990s saw the Mapuche fighting back and staging protests, occupying lands and destroying logging equipment. The government feared the influence of right-wing extremists, such as the Zapatistas in Mexico, and has led to the government agreeing to cancel debts, spending money on roads and schools, and to return large portions of land to the Mapuche, although that is yet to be seen.

Much of their culture lives on. They still speak Mapudungun – known as the language of the earth – in rural communities and in communal gatherings. They still participate in *mingakos* or communal works to help a member of the community during harvest time. *Rukas*, which are traditional wooden thatched roof houses, are still used by many families for meals. Musical instruments such as the *trutruca* and the *kultrun* are used during ceremonies and can be found in craft markets.

Life today

The Mapuche's name derives from the word *che* (people) and *mapu* (of the land) in Mapudungun. Numbering more than one million today, the Mapuche populate mostly the hills and mountains of La Araucanía, and can be seen wandering through the streets of Temuco and rural areas in the region, where the highest concentrations of their population exist. Their livelihood is based largely on agriculture and handicrafts, although many are migrating to the cities for work, where several hundred thousand live in squalor. Their education and unemployment levels tend to be out of sync with the rest of the country. There is hope, however; schools in Araucanía have begun teaching the Mapuche language and history in the hope of preserving it for future generations. To learn more about the Mapuche, visit *www.mapuche-nation.org*

Chiloé

Isolated from the mainland until the mid-19th century, the Chiloé archipelago evolved a culture unique from the rest of Chile. Distinct architecture, mythology, seafaring traditions and gastronomy combine to make a strange and fascinating charm. The island chain is made of more than 40 islands, dominated by the Isla Grande de Chiloé, which, at 180km (112 miles) long and 50km (31 miles) wide, is the second largest island in South America after Tierra del Fuego. A patchwork of farms dots the green hillsides. Quaint villages are centred around the island's distinguishing wooden churches. Of the 150, 16 have been declared UNESCO World Heritage Sites.

Chiloé was first inhabited by the Chono and later the Mapuche people. In 1567, the Spanish took control of the islands and disease quickly wiped out most of the indigenous population. Afterwards, the islands were the very last Spanish stronghold in Chile and didn't succumb until 1826. There is a strong sense of unity among the people here, and they still think of themselves as Chilotes, rather than Chileans.

Chiloé

Rowing in a Chiloé bay

Palafito houses, a protected national monument

CASTRO AND ANCUD
Castro

Rows of *palafito* (stilt) houses line the shores of Castro, the capital of Chiloé, making it the most well known and most distinctive village in the island chain. Set amid rolling hills and mist-covered bays, the small grid of streets has an other-worldly feel, characterised by the unusual architecture, roving street performers, artisans, fishermen and a strong tourist infrastructure. The *palafito* (stilt) houses line the estuary to the southwest, south and northeast of town, with several others scattered around. The colourful, wood-shingled houses serve as docks for local boats and have become one of the defining symbols of Chiloé. The largest clusters of these houses can be found here in Castro, and are protected national monuments.

Be sure to visit the Iglesia San Francisco, on the northeast corner of the plaza – it's pinkish aluminium with violet trim. The inside, completely wood from floor to ceiling with a number of interesting carvings, has been wonderfully restored. Erected in 1906, this church replaced several others that were burnt down. The market – both fresh produce and artisan – lines the area near the port and is surrounded with *palafito* (stilt) restaurants serving regional dishes such as *curanto* (meat, potato and shellfish stew). Shops around town sell brightly coloured liqueurs made from herbs, fruits and spices soaked in alcohol. *Licor de Oro* is the best known and combines milk, alcohol, sugar, cloves, lemons, saffron, almonds, vanilla and cinnamon – be prepared for an overwhelming attack on your taste buds.

Castro is the transport hub for much of the islands, and buses – often combined with ferries – head to any destination on the Isla Grande, as well as direct trips to many mainland cities.

Ancud

Ancud, the nearest large Chilote town from Puerto Montt, is the site of the last Spanish stronghold in Chile. It wasn't until January 1826 that the Spanish surrendered and only six days before the very last stronghold fell at the Port of Callao in Lima, Peru.

Fuerte San Antonio, built in 1770, dominates the town to the north, while a number of pleasant beaches can be found around the bay. Immaculate colonial-style buildings and *palafito* (stilt) houses once lined the city; however, a strong earthquake in 1960 destroyed much of the best architecture, and now only remnants of these older buildings can be seen. *Ancud is accessed by car ferry from Puerto Montt, or by bus from Castro.*

Fuerte San Antonio

This scenic Spanish fortress, built in 1770, was Spain's last foothold in Chile. Cannon emplacements can still be seen overlooking the harbour where the Spanish resisted heavy Criollo attacks in 1820 and 1824. *At the corner of Cochrane and Baquedano, a five-minute walk northwest of the centre.*

Museo Regional Aurelio Bórquez Candora

This is one of the best museums for the history of the islands and everything Chilote. Displays include artefacts from the original indigenous inhabitants, churches, Jesuits and a full-size replica of the *Ancud* – the ship that sailed south from Chiloé to claim Chile's southern territories. *Plaza de Armas, Libertad 370. Open: Jan–Feb Mon–Fri 10.30am–7.30pm, March–Dec Mon–Fri 9.30am–5.30pm, Sat–Sun 10am–2pm.*

Iglesia San Francisco in Castro

OTHER ATTRACTIONS ON CHILOE

Achao

Noted for its nationally recognised church and lively harbour, the seaside village of Achao is most often visited on a day trip from Castro. The restored Iglesia Santa María de Loreto, topped by a 25m (82ft) tower, is an 18th-century Jesuit church and is the oldest in Chiloé – it's also a UNESCO World Heritage Site. Note the alerce shingles of the church, which were fastened with wooden pegs, as opposed to nails. The market area near the docks is bustling most days of the week, with the largest markets on Monday, Wednesday and Friday. Villagers from the outlying islands come in by dinghy to sell their produce including cheeses, seaweed, tubers, peat moss (used for fuel) and *nalca*, a sea plant that is part of the local diet.

Fishing and passenger boats tied together in Achao

Achao is reached by a short car-ferry ride from the main island at Dalcahue.

Isla Lingua

A place lost in time, the tiny island is rarely visited by the outside world and it has remained unchanged by time. The century-old wooden church is the dominating feature. A unique form of basketry is produced by the locals, which can also be found in Achao. *Isla Lingua is reached by a 30-minute boat ride from Achao.*

Isla Quinchao

Quinchao, the second largest island in the chain, retains an air of traditional Chilote life, with green farmland and pastures covering the hills, wooden shingle houses and quaint seaside harbours. One paved road connects each end of the 25km- (15½-mile-) long island. *Isla Quinchao is reached by a short car ferry ride from the main island at Dalcahue.*

Parque Nacional de Chiloé

Covering a large section of the western coast of the Isla Grande, this 43,000ha (106,252-acre) national park is covered with rain-soaked evergreen forests and filled with diverse wildlife. One hundred and ten species of bird have been recorded, as well as foxes, sea lions and the pudú, a rare breed of deer. Small communities of the indigenous Huilliche live within the park's boundaries as well. The park is

Traditional wooden-shingle architecture in Achao

crisscrossed by a number of good hiking trails, while treks on horseback and kayaking trips may also be arranged.

The park is located one and a half hours by bus or taxi from the town of Chonchi, from where connections to Castro (30 minutes) can be made.

Pingüinera Puñihuil

Off the coast of the small cove of Puñihuil, there are a few small islets that are breeding grounds for Magellanic and Humboldt penguins, as well as several sea lion colonies. The penguins arrive in September, where they nest until March.

Tours on rubber Zodiac rafts can be arranged from Ancud travel agencies.

Quellón

Quellón is located at the end of Highway 5, otherwise known as the PanAmerican Highway. This busy port is the hub of the island's expanding shellfish and salmon farming industry, and the southern point for transport by ferry to the mainland. A number of *palafito* (stilt) houses line the banks of the town and are best seen from the water.

Quellón is reached by ferry from Chaitén in Northern Patagonia (six hours), or by bus from Castro (two hours).

Mythology in Chiloé

Native beliefs were intertwined with Catholicism to form the main structure of Chiloé's extensive mythology. The folklore of the island chain tells of creation myths, witches, gnomes and ghosts. Poor harvests and illness can be explained by many of the tales and by supposed interactions by the mythological creatures; as can cheating husbands, miscarriages and the creation of the land and the island chain's separation from the mainland. Many tales deal with life on the seas, lost fishermen, haunted ships and straying from clean living – still an important part of the world view of many Chilotes today.

Thousands of years ago the archipelago was attached to the mainland, and the serpent goddess of water, **Cai-Cai Vilú**, began a battle against the land, causing the waters to rise, burying the lowland areas and drowning many of the inhabitants. **Ten-Ten Vilú**, the serpent goddess of land, fought back against her opposite and enemy Cai-Cai, preventing her from covering the

Volcán Corcovado keeping watch on the island chain

Woodcarvings combining Christianity with local mythology

Invunche. The witches have the ability to fly, turn themselves into animals, raise sea levels and wipe out entire families due to illness.

El Caleuche is a glowing ship that appears while commercial vessels are lost in the fog and lures them closer by the enchanting singing and dancing of the *brujos* on board. The ship, possibly related to a Dutch pirate ship that once plied these waters, can travel at rapid speeds above or below the water.

Living in the woods, **Fiura** is a dreadfully ugly woman with foul breath, who dresses in moss. The spirit is an irresistible seductress, however, and single men are unable to resist her or her sexual appetite. Fiura's opposite is **Trauco**, a hideous, strong forest gnome who carries a stone axe and is found irresistible to young virgins, seducing them with a single glance. He is known to cause the girls to have a child out of wedlock.

Pincoya, is a long-haired goddess of extreme beauty and the personification of the ocean, and often saves stranded fishermen and sailors. The marine harvest depends on her actions. When Pincoya dances on the shore and faces the open sea, the harvest will be plentiful. If Pincoya faces the land, the harvest will be small.

island completely and saving its inhabitants. The damage had been done though, and the land became separated from the rest of the continent. The fight continued for hundreds of years, significantly altering the landscape of the chain. Mountain peaks and hills formed the islands. Valleys became inlets. Animals became rocks and people who didn't escape the water became seals and fish.

Other tales of struggles between good and evil direct islanders to pure living. *Brujos* (witches) are the centre of many of the legends. With their magical powers, these witches corrupt the good ways of life of many Chilotes. Their headquarters, called Recta Provincia, is thought to be in a cave near the town of Quicaví, guarded by the disfigured human

Northern Patagonia

The northern half of Patagonia remains as wild and isolated as its southern neighbour and feels even more remote. Glaciation has altered the landscape dramatically here. Tiny villages, which are scattered throughout the area, are set adjacent to raging rivers, waterfalls, glaciers, fiords, hot springs and old-growth forests.

Mountain biking the Carretera Austral

No roads connect the north to the rest of the country; only a few ferry routes run south to Puerto Natales, west to Chiloé and north to Puerto Montt. The Carretera Austral, which stretches from Chaitén in the north to Villa O'Higgins on the Argentine border in the south, was only built in the last couple of decades. Lately the region has become a hot spot for kayaking and fly-fishing, with some of the world's best operators bringing celebrities and a number of wealthy international visitors to this area with its untouched atmosphere.

PARQUE PUMALÍN AND ENVIRONS
Parque Pumalín

Parque Pumalín sums up Northern Patagonia better than words. The park covers 2,889sq km (1,115sq miles) from Hornopirén in the north to Chaitén in the south. Besides extensive forests, there are fiords, a sea-lion rookery and pristine scenery. A variety of eco projects are underway in the park, with aims of conservation and productivity, including animal husbandry, cheese making, ecotourism, wool handicrafts and organic gardens, which can be found at the park stations/visitor information centres. This private reserve has been the topic of controversy for the past few years: in 1991 American businessman Doug Tompkins, founder of North Face clothing, and his wife Kristine, a former CEO of the Patagonia clothing line, bought 16,997½ ha (42,000 acres) of evergreen forests to protect it from exploitation. A conservation land trust then added another 283,290ha (700,000 acres). Chileans feared that a swathe of land that stretched from the Pacific to the Argentine border, owned by an American businessman no less, would threaten their sovereignty. The land was donated to Fundación Pumalín (a Chilean foundation), which has eased the tension and it is hoped that this area will soon become a national park. *The park is entered from Hornopirén on the northern sector and from Chaitén in the south, which is the main entrance and has the most facilities. There is an information centre at 62 O'Higgins Street in Chaitén.*

Chaitén

This is a small fishing village and ferry port that connects Northern Patagonia to the rest of the country. Access to the southern portion of Parque Pumalín has led to a limited tourist influx during the summer, although the town is still relatively quiet. Just a few streets run parallel to the bay surrounded by green hills. The towering, snow-covered volcanoes of Michinmahuida and Corcovado can be seen in the northeast and southwest. *From Chaitén, ferries run north to Hornopirén and west to Quellón on the*

Chaitén at night

Waterfalls streaming down the mountain, due to the melting ice cap

Isla Grande de Chiloé, while buses link the city to places south of here.

Futaleufú

One of the world's best river rafting experiences is located here in Northern Patagonia, along the Argentine border. The Río Futaleufú attracts thousands of rafting and kayaking enthusiasts from across the world to experience a number of Class IV, V and V+ rapids – some of the world's most challenging – on a number of raging blue rivers amid dramatic mountain scenery. The village itself consists of a few dozen pastel-coloured houses, and serene lakeside cabins can be found in the areas around town.

Futaleufú is reached by bus from Chaitén (three and a half hours) or Puerto Montt (13 hours) via Argentina.

PARQUE NACIONAL LAGUNA SAN RAFAEL AND ENVIRONS

Coyhaique

Named after a Tehuelche word, *koi aike*, which means 'place of lakes', Coyhaique is set in a wide barren valley unlike much of the rest of mountainous and forest-covered Northern Patagonia. With roughly 50,000 residents, more than half the population of the entire region lives here. Tourist restaurants, hotels and a small indigenous artisan market surround a pentagonal-shaped main square.

Coyahaique is accessible by bus from Chaitén (11 hours) and by plane from Puerto Montt and Punta Arenas.

Parque Nacional Laguna San Rafael

This national park, full of rugged islands and fiords, extends 1,742,000ha (4,304,423 acres) across Northern Patagonia, 440,000ha (1,087,225 acres) of which comprise the Northern Ice Fields and its 19 glaciers. It was declared a UNESCO World Biosphere Reserve in 1978. Boat trips come to visit the San Rafael Glacier, a glowing blue block of ice rising directly out of the water. Pieces fall off and crash thunderously below. The largest peak in the southern Andes, Mount San Valentín (4,058m/13,314ft) sits on the eastern edge of the park.

Monument to sheep herding – wool is a major industry here

The park is located 120 marine miles southeast of Puerto Chacabuco, and reached by boat from Puerto Chacabuco and Puerto Natales.

Puerto Chacabuco

Green forested hills and snow-covered mountains rise right out of the water of this fly-fishing mecca set at the end of a narrow fiord. The mountains surrounding it are mostly unexplored and unscathed, making it one of the most immaculate settings in the region.

The frontier village is most often visited for its five-star resorts, visited by the international jet set and those en route to visit Laguna San Rafael National Park.

Puerto Chacabuco is reached by road from Coyhaique or ferries from the north or south.

Termas de Puyuhuapi

The luxury resort sits on the western shore of the Seno Ventisquero, surrounded by lush forests and misty lagoons. There are a number of indoor and outdoor pools ranging in temperature, and a full-scale spa with yoga, massages and seaweed treatments. The lodge is set on a private reserve in complete isolation.

The Termas can only be reached by boat from Bahía Dorita, just south of Puerto Puyuhuapi.

Villa O'Higgins

On the Argentine border, this is the end of the Carretera Austral. Set among

Windmills near Coyhaique

untamed, remarkable mountains and forests, it is most often explored on horseback. Although founded by English settlers in the early 20th century, it was only in 1999 that a road finally reached here. Just 450 residents of mixed ancestry live here today, but the road has opened up a growing tourist infrastructure.

Villa O'Higgins is seven hours south of Cochrane or one hour west of El Chaitén, Argentina by bus.

Drive: The Carretera Austral

Although not necessarily an economically sound idea, General Pinochet wanted to link some of the rainy, isolated fishing villages – reachable only by boat – to the rest of the country, and for that reason alone he has remained popular in the region. Work began in 1976, and is still only partially paved, although work is ongoing in many areas.

The lush, temperate rainforest is full of snow-covered peaks dripping with waterfalls, raging emerald rivers, falling rocks, and small, unspoiled villages that were virtually unknown before the road was complete. The trip can only be attempted during the summer months. It has become one of the world's legendary mountain biking trips as well, with more and more attempting the rough path each year. The 1,200km (745-mile) trip can be attempted in one day by car, although most will break up the journey, spending time in the quaint villages and resorts they pass along the way.

Day 1
Chaitén

A ferry from Hornopirén, near the entrance to the northern section of Parque Pumalín, will take you to Chaitén – a small fishing village and port, and capital of the Palena province. From here, buses head south through the vast forests along the Carretera Austral. Covered in mist for much of the year, it is surrounded by the superb natural beauty of the small, rocky bay that it sits on and the evergreen forests that surround it.

Day 2
La Junta

The first leg of the journey is categorised by extreme drops and climbs – one of the most difficult sections is by bike. Fly-fishing and rock climbing in Reserva Nacional Lago Rosselot and Lago Verde attract a number of visitors, and La Junta is a good place to break the journey or make transfers. A large sign and plaque, erected in 2000, marks the Carretera Austral and gives thanks to Pinochet for linking the town to the rest of the country.

Day 3
Puyuhuapi

With a pleasant harbour and access to Parque Nacional Queulat and the Termas de Puyuhuapi, Chile's most luxurious hot springs resort, Puyuhuapi is quickly attracting a larger crowd. The village, founded by Sudetan Germans after World War II, is just a small collection of aluminium-clad houses designed in German and Chilote architecture beside a narrow inlet filled with colourful handcrafted dinghies.

Day 4
Coyhaique

The road enters a wide valley at Coyhaique. Flat and full of farms and ranches, the area resembles nothing seen in the previous 11 hours of driving. With the good hotels and tourist facilities, it's a good place to rest for a day or spend some time fly-fishing in what is considered to be one of the world's best locations.

Day 5
Villa O'Higgins

The last leg of the journey from Cochrane to Villa O'Higgins passes through dense wilderness and can only be completed by using a car ferry. With a population of just 450 and only accessible by road since 1999, Villa O'Higgins is more or less where the road ends. Transport further south must be made by going into Argentina and back out near Puerto Natales.

Drive: The Carretera Austral

Scenery along the highway

Southern Patagonia

Locals call it El Fin del Mundo – the end of the world. Isolated by mountains and water from the rest of the mainland, Southern Patagonia contains some of the world's most dramatic terrain filled with a labyrinth of fiords, shimmering blue glaciers, islands, lush forests, fog and water looming in every direction.

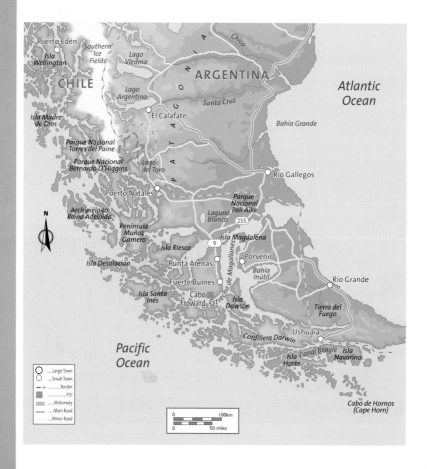

Parque Nacional Torres del Paine will be the highlight of any visit to Chile or the South American continent, but this region is loaded with numerous other incredible parks and abundant wildlife. A cast of characters has left the region rich in culture, from indigenous tribes to Antarctic explorers and waves of immigrants. The cities, once simply nothing more than backwater trading posts, have blossomed into major resorts where Gore-Tex is as common as *centolla* (king crab) fishermen. These cities are set amid towering, snow-covered mountains and strung out along major bodies of water filled with marine life, while any number of adventure activities can be arranged, including hiking, rafting, kayaking or climbing.

Hundreds of thousands of visitors now visit this region each year, compared to just a few thousand that made their way here annually a few decades ago. As the tourist infrastructure grows, more travellers are discovering the bounties of exploring this isolated region.

The Parque Nacional Torres del Paine is a UNESCO World Biosphere Reserve

PARQUE NACIONAL TORRES DEL PAINE

Named a UNESCO World Biosphere Reserve in 1978, Torres del Paine is the most likely reason anyone comes to Southern Patagonia and is one of the highlights of the continent. More than 200,000 annual visitors make their way to the 181,000ha (447,245-acre) park from across the globe for a photo trip by bus, wildlife watching, glacier spotting, multi-day hikes through the well maintained trail system, or to stay in some of the most magnificent nature lodges on the planet. The best time to visit is during the peak season (January–February) while the weather is best. However, the crowds are heavy and the *refugios* (nature lodges) must be booked well in advance. The rest of the year there are few other hikers and less wind, but the weather is far more unpredictable and can change from blue, sunny skies to ice and snow in a matter of minutes, which restricts many services and limits routes.

The Torres del Paine themselves include the granite pillars that rise like fingers more than 2,800m (9,186ft) above the windswept Patagonian steppe. Snow-capped Paine Grande (3,050m/10,007ft) sits to one side, while the black peaks of Los Cuernos (2,200–2,600m/7,218–8,530ft) sit to the other. The combination of magnificent peaks provides endless photo opportunities. The Torres form the centre of the park while the roads and trails have been constructed in a circle around them.

If you are hiking, the park has more than 250km (155 miles) of well-marked trails. There is a good chance though it will be the 'W' hike (*see p110*), a four-

Waterfall from a melting ice cap

Guanacos in front of the Torres del Paine

to five-day, 76.1km (47¼-mile) trek across some of the most stunning terrain anywhere, which, on a map, looks like a 'W'. The 93.2km (58-mile) circuit is even more challenging and takes anywhere from seven to nine days. There are also boat rides to the glaciers, rides to the park, and some of the most striking resorts in the world. This is the heart of the area's wild and windswept countryside, which abounds with lush forest, cool blue glaciers, abundant wildlife and awe-inspiring views from every angle.

CONAF Visitors' Centre and Parque Administración

The visitors' centre has a wide variety of information on the park, from maps to wildlife displays and a birdwatching balcony. Every visitor to the park receives a free map that displays detailed information on hiking trails such as the 'W', distances between lodges and campsites, rules, advice and other amenities located in the park.

Open: 8.30am–8pm. Located at Lago del Toro, across from Posada Río Serrano.

The park is accessible by bus or taxi from Puerto Natales (one to two-and-a-half hours) and from El Calafate, Argentina. Another option is to take a tour bus from Puerto Natales, which drives by many of the park's highlights, stopping for lunch at a refuge, and returning to Puerto Natales the same night. Boats and ferries enter the park from the south from Puerto Natales, stopping at glaciers Balmaceda and Serrano and then transferring to a speedboat up the Río Serrano. From within the park, several bus companies run from the Parque Administración office to Puerto Natales, stopping at Laguna Amarga and Lago Pehoé. Admission: $18,000 pesos per person. If climbing, an additional permit is required from the Dirección de Fronteras y Límites in Santiago (*www.difrol.cl*), which should be requested well in advance.

Walk: The 'W'

This famous 76.1km (47¼-mile) walk is at the top of every hiker's resumé and is becoming more crowded each year. The route combines the most dramatic scenery found within the park, while avoiding the most difficult sections of the circuit. Thousands attempt at least some part of the hike each day. The hike, named after the 'W' shape of the route, takes you between the Cuernos and up the mountain valleys, right up to the Torres del Paine, passing serene alpine lakes, herds of guanaco and a plethora of other wildlife.

Campgrounds and lodges are scattered at the beginning and end of each hike, about four hours apart, which give you access to hot showers and great meals from anywhere on the trek, although most can only afford what comes off their camping stove. Anyone can attempt the hike, which is only of mid-level difficulty at a few points, and points of return are easily accessible if one needs to turn around due to weather or lack of physical fitness. Sufficient maps are available from the Parque Administración office, which provides major details of the hike, although a number of more

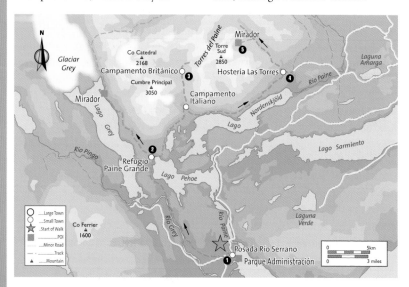

detailed ones can be found in Puerto Natales, especially good if you plan on attempting lesser-known trails.

Day 1 end point
Refugio Paine Grande

Most will begin east to west from the Parque Administración office near the Posada Río Serrano, which offers plenty of useful information. You will first walk a flat and simple five hours by the side of Río Grey to the campsite at Refugio Paine Grande.

Day 2 end point
Refugio Paine Grande

From here you leave your gear and take a light bag for a three-hour walk each way through grassy land above Lago Grey, passing lakes and fields of wildflowers. You will end at the mirador next to Glacier Grey, where you will get very close to the glacier and see a number of radiant blue icebergs

Parque Nacional Torres del Paine; hiking to the glacier

floating in the water below, before returning back to camp by nightfall.

Day 3 end point
Campamento Británico or Italiano

From Refugio Paine Grande you make your way two hours east to Valley Frances. From Campamento Italiano, where you may camp, you will climb inland a scenic five hours between Paine Grande and the Torres del Paine, not to mention a number of glaciers. You will begin your return about one hour beyond Campo Británico, where you can also camp. Which campsite you return to determines how far you will walk the next day.

Day 4 end point
Hostería Las Torres

From Campamento Italiano it will take about five to seven hours, past the eastern face of the Torres del Paine and one of the best photo opportunities available, to reach Hostería Las Torres. The walk is fairly easy and closely follows Lago Nordenskjöld.

Day 5 end point
Puerto Natales or Hostería Las Torres

The last day involves a round trip trek from the campground to the mirador, which is about four hours each way. This can be bitterly cold and snowy during winter. There are campsites scattered along this trail if you wish to stick around for a few more days; however, most come back down for transport out of the park.

Walk: The 'W'

Patagonia wildlife

With dozens of national parks in Patagonia, it is little wonder that wildlife is abundant here. Protection is heavily enforced and numbers of creatures that were once dwindling now thrive. Many of the creatures, isolated by mountains and water, are endemic to the small sections of the Andes range and relatively unknown to international tourists.

The Patagonia region, particularly in Parque Nacional Torres del Paine, is home to herds of **guanacos**, which

Rhea or ñandú

once were threatened in the park, but now thrive due to a well-executed conservation effort. They are quite tame, often stopping to stare at tour buses, seemingly posing for photos. This camelid is similar to the llama or alpaca with thinner legs and longer neck. It exists mostly in high altitude areas and is found only in the extreme north and south of the country.

A number of other mammal species are found throughout the region. The **Patagonia puma**, although rarely seen, is one of the largest of the 27 puma subspecies. It thrives on guanaco in Parque Nacional Torres del Paine, where it has a large presence. Also on hand are the **red** and **grey foxes** and the **pudú**, an elusive deer that lives only in thick-forested areas.

Bird life is some of the most interesting on the planet. The **rhea**, called the *ñandú* in Spanish, is a tall, flightless bird that travels in small packs and is often seen along the roadways amid high shrubbery or along the Patagonia plains or Altiplano in the north. It resembles an ostrich, but is slightly smaller and has three toes instead of two. The **Andean condor**, sacred to many indigenous cultures, has a wingspan

Seno Otway Magellanic penguins

that can reach up to 3m (10ft). Although becoming increasingly rare in other parts of the Andes, it is often seen throughout Patagonia in the early morning and afternoon rising above the warm thermals.

Several species of **flamingo** can be found in high-altitude lakes, in large nesting colonies, throughout the south.

Marine life is perhaps the most astounding aspect any visitor will remember from Patagonia, particularly if heading to the southernmost regions. **Magellanic** and **Humboldt penguin** colonies are sprinkled across the region, with several located within easy reach of Punta Arenas. The birds build their nests in the tens of thousands in small burrows along the windswept shores. **Sea lions**, **elephant seals** and **fur seals** maintain colonies as well, best seen during the October to December breeding season.

In the water, a number of whale and dolphin species can be seen. **Commerson's dolphin** is one of the most common, while the rare **hourglass dolphin** and the **Chilean dolphin** are found mostly around Cape Horn. **Fin**, **humpback**, **orcas** and **blue whales** can all be seen in the icy waters of Patagonia. A very rare blue whale nursery was located in 2003 to the southeast of Chiloé, which many hope will become a marine reserve in the near future.

Boat trip: Chilean fiords

Once just a shipping route for Navimag ferries, this trip through Chile's glacier-filled fiords has become one of the most highly sought-after cruises in the world, with an itinerary that rivals any Carnival or Royal Caribbean Cruise ship.

The three-day/four-night trip stops at several sites, isolated by freezing waters and snowy mountains, which cannot otherwise be visited. A range of accommodation is available, and prices fall dramatically outside of the December–March high season. Although prices may be low in the winter, little can be seen if the weather is bad and the seas tend to be considerably rougher. Most stick to C-berth cabins during the summer, which are little more than dorms with shared bathrooms, but include meals, talks and on-board activities. First-class AAA cabins have just a couple of bunks, a writing desk and the best views on the ship.

Departure point heading north to south

Puerto Montt

Founded in 1853 and home to a number of German immigrants, *palafito* (stilt) houses and an abundance of regional seafood dishes, Puerto Montt is the capital of Chile's Lakes District. The bustling fish market and traditional craft stalls and restaurants that line the Angelmó village to the west of the port is one of the most interesting aspects of the city. It gains considerable cultural and culinary influence from the mysterious island of Chiloé, which is a short ferry ride away.

First stop

Parque Nacional Laguna San Rafael

From Puerto Chacabuco, a ferry port and resort area where some of the world's best fly-fishing is done, there is access to Parque Nacional Laguna San Rafael. Declared a UNESCO World Biosphere Reserve in 1978, the park is home to the 440,000ha (1,087,225-acre) Northern Ice Fields. Melting at the base, the San Rafael Glacier is the highlight, as enormous blocks of ice noisily fall off into the sea. It is one of the last remnants of the Northern Ice Fields and the world's most equatorial sea-level glacier.

Second stop
Puerto Edén

The extremely isolated port is home to the surviving population of Kaweskar or Alacalufe native Indians, once nomadic groups who are now mussel fishermen. The fishermen who greet passengers offer visits to Malacca Bay, Angostura Inglesa and the shipwrecks. This is the only point of disembarkation on the cruise, and the only transport to the port other than by private boat.

Third stop
Southern Ice Fields

From 1 November to 30 March, the boats pass through the Southern Ice Fields, the third largest freshwater reserve in the world, where it's possible to see one of Chile's two most important glaciers. At 6km (3¾ miles) wide and 75m (246ft) high, Pio XI (on trips from north to south) is the largest glacier in the southern hemisphere. Amalia Glacier (south to north) is equally impressive at 1km (⅔ mile) wide and 40m (131ft) high.

End point
Puerto Natales

The end of the trip lands the boat at Puerto Natales on the shore of Seno Última Esperanza, where trips into Parque Nacional Torres del Paine or further south in Southern Patagonia, Tierra del Fuego and Antarctica are made.

Icebergs are a common sight in this region

PARQUE NACIONAL BERNARDO O'HIGGINS AND ENVIRONS
Cueva del Milodón

The Milodón, a giant ground sloth (*Mylodon listai*), inhabited Southern Patagonia as far back as 9,000 years ago. The partial remains of one of the creatures was found by German explorer Herman Eberhard in 1895 in what has become known as the Cueva del Milodón. Five years later, a Swedish expedition team sent the remains to Europe, where they are still housed in London's Natural History Museum. The excellent condition of the skin and the droppings of the Milodón led scientists to believe that the creatures may still be living in the area, so journalists and explorers went off in search of them with the aim of bringing some back for exhibition in British zoos. Of course they had no luck, but assembled a wealth of information on the area. The cave itself is filled with stalactites and stalagmites and surrounded by lush, temperate forests.

The cave is located 16km (10 miles) from Puerto Natales on the road to Torres del Paine and is reachable by bus, although it is often included in day tours of the national park. Admission charge.

Parque Nacional Bernardo O'Higgins

Not nearly as well known as its nearby neighbour Parque Nacional Torres del Paine, this park is just as majestic. There are a number of excellent trails, far fewer visitors, and boat trips to last a lifetime. Most will enter the park on a day ferry tour from Puerto Natales on the *21 de Mayo* cutter, with the main purpose of seeing the Balmaceda and Serrano glaciers. The bluer, larger Serrano Glacier is far more interesting and there is a short trail that leads near to its base, where kayaks and motorised dinghies can be hired to get up close. A *parrillada* (mixed grill) lunch and a trip to a sea lion colony or cattle ranch are generally included as part of the trip.

The park is reachable by a four- to six-hour ferry from Puerto Natales or a one-hour speedboat ride on the Río Serrano from Parque Nacional Torres del Paine.

Replica of a milodón

Seno Última Esperanza outside Puerto Natales

Puerto Natales

Puerto Natales is the gateway to Torres del Paine and ferry trips through the fiords take visitors through the jaw-dropping Seno de la Última Esperanza or 'Gulf of Last Hope', named after the last-ditch effort by Spanish explorer Juan Ladrilleros to find a route to the Magellan Strait.

The town was founded in 1908 by the Sociedad Explotadora de Tierra del Fuego, which bought the land several years earlier and erected a meat-packing plant. It's a small town, easily navigable by foot, and home to a thriving tourist population and infrastructure. Any number of excursions can be made into the area's national parks, and there are plenty of opportunities for adventure sport activities.

Puerto Natales is three hours northwest of Punta Arenas or five–six hours south of El Calafate, Argentina, by bus.

PUNTA ARENAS AND ENVIRONS
Punta Arenas

Located on a broad plain on the Magellan Strait, the town is defined by the lavish mansions built by wool and shipping barons, which have been restored to make hotels, museums and banks. Punta Arenas first blossomed into a supply centre for ships rounding Cabo de Hornos and heading north to California during the gold rush. Between 1890 and World War I a few hundred sheep were brought over from the Falkland Islands and just decades later there were millions of them as well as immigrant labourers – particularly Chilotes and Croats – who moved to the city in droves to work in the newly created *estancias* (farming estates), turning Punta Arenas into the largest city in Southern Patagonia. Be sure to walk to the top of Cerro La Cruz, a ten-minute walk northwest of the centre, where you can see sweeping views of the city and the Strait.

Punta Arenas is reachable only by regional buses and ferries, and by air from Puerto Montt and Santiago. The city is 20 minutes from Carlos Ibáñez del Campo airport.

Sernatur (Tourist Information Office)
Waldo Seguel 989. Tel: 61-241-330. Open: Dec–Feb Mon–Fri 8.15am–8pm, Mar–Nov Mon–Fri 8.15am–6.45pm.

Cementerio Municipal
Stunning in both architecture and shrubbery, here you'll find the extravagant mausoleums of wealthy

View of Punta Arenas and the Strait of Magellan from Cerro La Cruz

that were previously unheard of in this barren, tin-roofed city. It is now the home to the Club de la Unión and Hotel José Nogueira.

Magallanes 949 on the plaza.
Tel: 061-244-216. Open: Dec–Feb daily
10.30am–5pm, Mar–Nov daily
10.30am–2pm. Admission charge.

Restored building of a shipping baron, now a bank

immigrant families, including the lavish tombs of José Menéndez, José Nogueira, Sara Braun and many Scots, Welsh, Croats, Germans and Scandinavians. There are interesting monuments to the Selk'nam (Ona) Indians and Germans that died in the Falklands War.

Five minutes northeast of the plaza
at Av Bulnes 949.

Palacio Mauricio Braun

This mansion belonging to sheep farmer Mauricio Braun, with its French furniture and other imported antiques, is one of the best examples of the extreme wealth that once swept over Punta Arenas. The house was designed by French architect Numa Mayer, who applied contemporary Parisian styles

Fuerte Bulnes and Cabo Froward

The barren, windswept cliffs along the southern points of the Magellan Strait are the very ends of the continent's mainland. The first and only settlements on this barren stretch of land, which were military garrisons, ended disastrously as the winter weather made the place uninhabitable. In 1843, sent by Chilean President Manuel Bulnes and captained by an ex-English officer and crewed by Chilotes, a ship sailed from Puerto Montt. The crew built a camp 60km (37 miles) south of Punta Arenas to claim the land for Chile, which several other countries were also en route to do. Cabo Froward is a further 30km (18 miles) at the very tip of the American continent. An enormous cross stands on a 365m (1,198-ft) hill, erected in 1913 by Señor Fagnano, and again in 1987 when the late Pope John Paul II visited. The wind here is incredible, making the two-day hike here quite challenging.

Several tour companies make the journey
to Fuerte Bulnes from Punta Arenas.
The cape is visited by a two-day hike
from the fort.

Magellanic penguins in Southern Patagonia

PENGUIN COLONIES AND PARQUE NACIONAL PALI AIKE
Penguin colonies
Isla Magdalena penguin colony

The Monumento Natural de los Pingüinos is where roughly 100,000 Magellanic penguins make their nests from September to March, before heading to Brazil in April. Be sure to check out the small lighthouse, dating to 1902, which gives the best views of the colony. The island sits in the middle of the Magellan Strait, a place of strong winds and home to numerous marine mammals that you are likely to see along the way.

The island, 35km (22 miles) north of Punta Arenas, is reachable only by tour boat from Punta Arenas in good weather. Admission charge.

Seno Otway penguin colony

This smaller and slightly less impressive 80ha (198-acre) park is home to about 10,000 Magellanic penguins and is one of the most popular day trips from Punta Arenas. The birds nest in small holes in the ground and waddle back and forth from the nearby beach to feed their young. En route to the colony you may see rheas, Patagonian hares, skunks and numerous birds.

65km (40 miles) north of Punta Arenas
reachable by bus or private tour.
Admission charge.

Parque Nacional Pali Aike

Sitting just before the Argentine border
200km (124 miles) northeast of Punta
Arenas, this 5,030ha (12,429-acre) park
consists mainly of volcanic steppe with a
number of hiking trails across sharp lava
beds inhabited by guanacos, ñandúes,
armadillos, skunks and foxes.

Excavations from Pali Aike cave, a lava
tube in the park, in the 1930s yielded the
remains of the milodón (giant ground
sloth), *onohippidium* (a native horse)
and primitive human settlements.
No public transport; frequent tours depart
from Punta Arenas. Admission charge.

BRUCE CHATWIN, IN PATAGONIA

It was a hairy, orange piece of skin from
a giant sloth, an animal extinct for thousands
of years, set in a glass cabinet at his
grandmother's house in England that
fascinated writer Bruce Chatwin as a child.
Years later, the memory of the artefact
inspired him to visit Patagonia on a
six-month jaunt in his thirties. The skin was
sent by his eccentric uncle, Charley Milward,
who lived in Punta Arenas. His house,
known as Castillo Milward, can still be
seen at España 959.

Chatwin's *In Patagonia*, published in 1977,
is still the premier travelogue on the region
today. It was based largely on Milward's life
and the author's experiences here with his
uncle and the fascinating array of characters
such as outlaws and displaced immigrant
communities that inhabited Patagonia
at the time.

Around 100,000 Magellanic penguins nest on Isla Magdalena

Southern Patagonia

TIERRA DEL FUEGO

This island – the largest in South America – is split between Argentina and Chile. Although the Ushuaia section of the island is well known on the tourist map, the Chilean version is still a place of bird colonies, farmland and historical sights seen only by the extremely curious. The northern half is a barren plain full of sheep farms, while the southern half is more wild, ranging from the Cordillera Darwin, with snow-covered mountains rising right out of the sea, to flowering meadows and false beech forests. The island was nicknamed Tierra del Humo meaning 'land of smoke' by Ferdinand Magellan because of the smoke from the small fires that the indigenous inhabitants lit across the hillsides to keep warm. It was later altered to Tierra del Fuego, meaning 'land of fire'.

Porvenir

Porvenir is the largest city in the Chilean part of Tierra del Fuego and was founded in 1883 during the area's gold rush. This frontier town sits on a wide plain on the Magellan Strait, looking across to Punta Arenas. It is home to metal-clad Victorian houses, a few good seafood restaurants, a dolphin-filled bay and typical 1920s architecture of the area. Gold, fishing and sheep farming have brought an interesting mix of immigrants, mostly Croatians and Chilotes. Tours can be arranged in town to nearby villages, bays and *estancias* (farming estates), which are a good way to see hard, unspoiled Fuegian life.

The town covers roughly 20,000ha (49,419 acres) of rural land with sheep *estancias* for producing wool, as well as cattle farms and breeding facilities

Marine birds on the old dock at Porvenir

The windswept shore of Tierra del Fuego

including some for race horses that are ecologically bred without the use of chemicals or hormones. The Bahía Chilota Lighthouse sits 8km (5 miles) to the south. Fishing in nearby Lago Blanco is quite popular, as is fly-fishing in the town's many rivers and streams.

Fernando Cordero Rusque Museum

One of the most visited sites in the city, particularly by those on day trips from Punta Arenas, this museum is best known for its displays on the Selk'nam indigenous group – particularly its collection of skulls, mummies and photographs. There's also an assortment of local flora and fauna, exhibits on the gold rush, and Porvenir's small film industry, which dates back to the early 20th century. *On the plaza at 402 Calle Padre Mario Zavatero. Tel: 61-580-094. Open: Mon–Fri 9am–5pm, Sat–Sun 10.30am–1.30pm & 3–5pm. Admission charge.*

Porvenir and Tierra del Fuego are accessible by a daily ferry service from Punta Arenas or by bus from the Argentine side of the island.

CABO DE HORNOS AND
THE SOUTH
Cabo de Hornos (Cape Horn)

Rising 424m (1,391ft) out of the rough, icy waters stands the cape, flanked by imposing black cliffs. The island is covered by mosses and grasses and is home to just a few permanent residents. Wildlife is abundant, with Magellanic penguins on the southeastern shore, dolphins and whales just offshore, and a number of birds such as condors and albatrosses seen on occasion. Discovered by the Dutch in 1616, the uninhabited Cabos de Hornos island chains are the very last pieces of land before Antarctica.

Before the Panama Canal was built, rounding the cape was the quickest route from the east coast of the United States to the west, and became busiest during the California Gold Rush. *Flights from Puerto Williams to Cabo de Hornos, and boat trips on the Mare Australis from Puerto Natales, are available infrequently during the summer months.*

Isla Navarino

Isla Navarino is actually further south than Argentina's Ushuaia (which is marketed as 'the last town on earth'). Set on the other side of the Beagle Channel, technically it is considered part of Chilean Antarctica, although the terrain is dense forest, bogs and lakes. The island was once home to Yámana Canoe Indians who were wiped out by diseases brought by white settlers.

Wildlife is pristine here with an abundance of guanaco and plenty of bird life. The Canadian beaver has become somewhat of a nuisance and the government is paying trappers to help control the population – hence, they are now showing up on every restaurant menu. The Dientes de Navarino mountain chain is often considered more impressive than the Torres del Paine, and there are a number of good hikes easily accessed from Puerto Williams, including a 53.5km (33-mile) circuit.

Puerto Williams

On the north coast of Isla Navarino and officially the last settlement in the world before Antarctica, Puerto Williams is mostly a small naval base, although the seasonal *centolla* (king crab) fishermen are here and the burgeoning tourist population is inviting many others to stick around. The original bow of Shackleton's 1916 Antarctic voyage, the *Yelcho* can be seen at the entrance to the base. The town maintains the last remnants of the Yahgan Indians, of which about 50 remain and only a handful speak the language. There is a traditional house with handicraft demonstrations, called Kip-Akar, 15 minutes east along the shore.

Infrequent flights with Aerovías DAP are available from Punta Arenas (check at their office in the airport) and ferry service or passage by private yacht from Ushuaia, Argentina, are the only ways to reach Isla Navarino. Check in travel agencies or the Navimag ferry office in Ushuaia for more information on yachts or cruises.

Territorio Chileno Antártico

A pie wedge of the Antarctic continent has been claimed by Chile, although not officially recognised by the international community. It's a serene setting surrounded by whiteness. It is home to fabulous marine life and millions of Papua penguins and sea lion colonies. There is little snow in the summer and conditions are actually bearable, however, it can be very wet. Presidente Eduardo Frei Station was built in 1969 on the Fildes peninsula. There are no permanent residents, only a rotating population of scientists and military personnel, as well as a Correos de Chile Post Office.

Access is provided via expensive one- and two-day tours from Aerovías DAP in Punta Arenas.

A seagull near Cabo de Hornos

Chile's glaciers

With the towering peaks of the Andes running the length of the country along the eastern side, and the Antarctic to the south, Chile is a country where seeing a glacier is quite accessible. The highest concentrations are found in what are considered to be the Northern and Southern Ice Fields, best seen on the route through the fiords from Puerto Natales to Puerto Montt, and vice versa.

The Campo del Hielo Sur, or Southern Ice Fields, crossing both Chile and Argentina, hold 48 major glaciers and cover an area of more than 11,000sq km (4,250sq miles). Much of the ice fields are largely unexplored, with many studies made and recorded by aerial photographs only.

In Parque Nacional Bernardo O'Higgins, at 1,265sq km (488sq miles), the Pio XI Glacier is the largest in the southern hemisphere outside of Antarctica. Also known as the Brüggen Glacier, it has advanced significantly since 1945, moving more than 5km (3 miles) across the Eyre Fiord by 1976 and cutting off Lake Greve from the ocean. A number of more accessible glaciers within the park, such as Balmaceda

Hikers at Serrano Glacier

and Serrano can be seen by boat from Puerto Natales, which is one of the most popular one-day excursions in the region.

In Parque Nacional Torres del Paine, numerous glaciers can be seen. Glacier Grey is the most accessible, with a network of roads and footpaths leading directly to it. There's even an ecolodge set within view of it. A number of other glaciers, such as Tyndall, can also be seen on various hikes within the park. At the

258sq km (100sq miles) Perito Moreno Glacier, near El Calafate, Argentina, reached on a one-day trip from Puerto Natales and often combined with visits to Torres del Paine, is a beautiful blue block where the sounds of the ice cracking and falling into the water is an experience that few can forget.

Elsewhere, Parque Nacional San Rafael, reached by catamaran from Puerto Chacabuco in Northern Patagonia near Coyhaique, contains the entire Northern Ice Fields. It is a remnant of the larger Patagonia Ice Fields that covered much of the lower part of the continent tens of millions of years ago. It is still the largest ice mass beyond the polar regions and only survives due to its high elevation and a cool, moist marine climate. The azure blue San Rafael Glacier is without a doubt the highlight – it nearly reaches sea level and flows at 17m (56ft) a day, making it the world's fastest moving glacier.

Like the peak of Kilimanjaro in Tanzania, many of the glaciers are retreating and melting at alarming rates. Although they have remained relatively stable during the past 5,000 years, in the last 100 years the surface areas have been dramatically reduced. The San Rafael Glacier, for instance, has retreated more than a kilometre from where it was just over a decade ago. Global warming is believed to be the cause and, although the ice fields will not completely disappear for a very long time, we are only just beginning to understand the effects of this gradual change.

Glacier Grey, one of the glaciers to be seen in Parque Nacional Torres del Paine

Getting away from it all

Although sitting nowhere near the mainland, and with cultures all of their own, several palm-laden island jewels of the South Pacific are actually part of Chile. These are some of the most isolated places on earth, with beautiful, white sandy beaches that sit practically empty.

Archipiélago Juan Fernández

This tiny island chain, nearly 700km (435 miles) west of Valparaíso is both a national park and a World Biosphere Reserve. The 93sq km (36sq mile) Isla Robinson Crusoe is the largest of the islands and was where Scotsman Alexander Selkirk was marooned for four years, after a dispute with a ship captain. Daniel Defoe based his

Distance signs in Punta Arenas

legendary tale *Robinson Crusoe* on the lives of Selkirk and Friday, who was actually a Nicaraguan Miskito Indian called Will and was stranded on the island at a different time.

Fewer than 100 tourists visit these islands each month, spending their time between the main town of San Juan Bautista and the national park, which makes up every other inch of Isla Robinson Crusoe. Easy hiking trails cover much of the park and lead to the Mirador de Selkirk, which was where Selkirk scanned the horizon for approaching ships.

The park is also home to the Juan Fernández fur seal, of which fewer than 10,000 now exist, as well as many rare and endemic plants.
The island can be reached by plane from Santiago.

Easter Island

Also known as Isla de Pascua in Spanish or Rapa Nui in Polynesia, perhaps no island culture is as

Easter Island *Moai*

(2,237 miles) west of continental Chile and 2,075km (1,290 miles) east of tiny Pitcairn Island. Easter Island can be reached by plane from Santiago or Tahiti.

In the north

In the northern half of the country skies are clear and blue, while the earth takes on the calmness of the desert. The settlements are few and far between and only in the major ports are you reminded of civilisation. However, the Atacama Desert isn't empty: here you can find lush green valleys, vineyards and wildlife sanctuaries set beside volcanoes and sand dunes.

Bahía Inglesa

This beautiful bay with clear turquoise water was once favoured by British privateers. It has white sands, small waves and warm waters and is a windsurfing hotspot. A few excellent seafood restaurants and dome-shaped hotel rooms make up the small resort, which is one of the smallest and most serene and isolated in the country.

Parque Nacional Lauca

The Chilean Altiplano is a world away from the ports and modern cities of the rest of the Norte Chico. Parque Nacional Lauca is a UNESCO Biosphere Reserve set between Arica and La Paz, Bolivia, and is home to herds of vicuña and guanaco, vizcacha, rheas, condors and numerous other rare animal and bird species. Visitors

mysterious as this. The lush, green, lonely speck of land in the middle of the Pacific is covered in hundreds of *Moai* – giant stone statues that are well known around the world and set on *ahu* (platforms) – carved by skilled artisans. Little is known about how the statues were moved or raised. The island is made of three volcanoes and one small town, made up of just over 3,000 people. The natives were thought to have arrived by the Marquesas Islands in the 4th or 5th centuries. It's also one of the adventure capitals of the South Pacific, with surfing, scuba diving, hiking and horse riding available on many parts of the island. It is considered to be the most isolated island in the world, located 3,600km

The sun setting over Bahía Inglesa

make their way by road through the park past unspoiled Aymara villages to see dazzling Lago Chungará, with Volcán Parinacota looming behind it.

San Pedro de Atacama

The *adobe* (mud) village of San Pedro de Atacama is an oasis in the dry desert and the centre of an area full of natural sights. Bubbling and spitting geysers, a lunar-like landscape in the Valle de la Luna, and the largest salt lake in the country are a short drive away.

In the south

The regions south of Santiago are lush and green for much of the year, while snowfall isolates other parts during the rest. Some of the most dramatic landscapes in the world, with snow-capped peaks, glaciers, fiords, forests,

islands and wildlife reserves are found in this incredible region that has attracted adventurers for centuries.

Isla Navarino

If you don't feel away here, you never will. The southernmost permanently inhabited place on earth – even further than Tierra del Fuego – Isla Navarino is known for its dramatic, windswept landscapes known mostly to passing boats. Hike across lagoons, forests and mountains on the Dientes de Navarino circuit or go sea kayaking to sea bird habitats just short of Cabo de Hornos.

Parque Nacional Torres del Paine

If you want to get away in style, there's no better place than Parque Nacional Torres del Paine. You can spend a day hiking and then come back to one of the most luxurious *refugios* (nature lodges) in the world, with hot water showers and gourmet meals, completely isolated and sitting beside azure blue lakes and glaciers. The plush Hotel Explora (*Tel: 2-206-6060, www.explora.com*) on Lago Pehoé, is believed by many to be the top refugio in the world. Providing complete comfort, stunning design, a luxury spa and world-class food, the setting is incomparable.

Parque Nacional Vicente Rosales

One of Chile's oldest and most popular national parks, Vicente Rosales is 60km (37 miles) from Puerto Varas, in one of the most beautiful settings in the Lakes District. Hiking trails cross paths with several stunning volcanoes and are matched by sailing on the lime green waters of Lago Todos los Santos. From here you can visit lava tubes created by the eruption of Volcán Osorno in 1850, waterfalls and thermal baths.

Parque Pumalín

A major conservation effort from North Face clothing founder Doug Tompkins, stretching from the Pacific to almost the Argentine border, Parque Pumalín is the place to go for unspoiled scenery set around an eco-friendly infrastructure. This Northern Patagonia Park has caught the attention of nature reserves around the world, and is on the fast track to becoming a national park. You can hike or kayak past sea lion and penguin colonies by day, and soak in a hot spring after an organic dinner by nightfall.

Valle de la Luna, 'Valley of the Moon'

When to go

Covering more latitudinal ground than any other country, variations in weather tend to be many. At any given time, Chile offers a range of climates with changes being more extreme as you move from north to south. In general, the north, a temperate desert, although warm during the day can be bitterly cold at night. The central regions enjoy a Mediterranean climate for much of the year. In the south you must prepare for extreme weather that even in the summer can change from sun to snow within minutes.

Summer

The warmest weather is during the summer months of December to February. Many of the more isolated regions in the south are fully accessible only at this time, and the water is warm enough for swimming only in summer. However, prices are often doubled, hotels and buses are full and major tourist destinations are plagued by severe overcrowding. It's the Chilean holiday season so Santiago tends to evacuate. The north and central regions tend to be hot and humid, perfect for enjoying the beach resorts. It can get cool at night, particularly the closer you move to the Andes. In the far north this is the Bolivian or Altiplano Winter, when the Altiplano sees the most rain and some roads can be washed out. The Lakes District is hot as well, though furious but usually brief rain showers do occur. Patagonia tends to be warm during the day, with temperatures rising by as much as 20°C (68°F). It can rain at any time, though, and even snow in mountain

areas. The winds tend to be vicious most of the time. Daylight can last until midnight in the extreme south. This is the only time of year one can drive the Carretera Austral (*see pp104–5*).

Autumn

During autumn, from late February to May, the weather is cool throughout most of the country. The crowds tend to disappear and hotel rates tend to drop. This is the shoulder season and one of the best times to visit. In Patagonia, there is less wind and rain than in the summer, which makes this a good time to visit Torres del Paine or other national parks and natural sights.

Winter

For skiing, June to September are the best months. Many mountain passes, rural roads and border crossings into Argentina are impassable due to snow. The northern Altiplano and Parque Nacional Lauca see virtually no rain at this time, while the Lakes District is crisp and cool, but rarely drops below 10°C (50°F). In Patagonia, the weather is less predictable, and sunshine and blue skies can suddenly change to high winds, rain and snow. Some hiking routes and parts of Torres del Paine may be closed down. However, many still visit and may experience weeks of clear weather.

Spring

From October to November the weather tends to be mild, and crowds are nowhere to be found. In the central regions the weather is cool and wet, while the north stays dry. Patagonia is unpredictable and you can see four seasons in a day. The ozone hole over Patagonia tends to cause the worst ultraviolet radiation at this time, so high-factor sun cream and UV-protected sunglasses are a must.

When to go

WEATHER CONVERSION CHART

25.4mm = 1 inch
°F = 1.8 × °C + 32

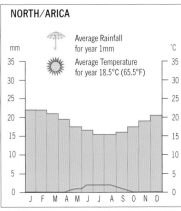

NORTH/ARICA

Average Rainfall for year 1mm

Average Temperature for year 18.5°C (65.5°F)

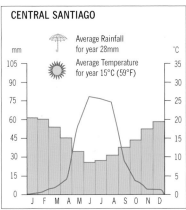

CENTRAL SANTIAGO

Average Rainfall for year 28mm

Average Temperature for year 15°C (59°F)

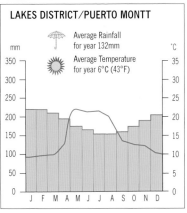

LAKES DISTRICT/PUERTO MONTT

Average Rainfall for year 132mm

Average Temperature for year 6°C (43°F)

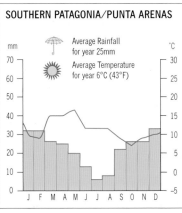

SOUTHERN PATAGONIA/PUNTA ARENAS

Average Rainfall for year 25mm

Average Temperature for year 6°C (43°F)

Getting around

Chilean public transport is surprisingly reliable and comfortable compared with other Latin American nations. For longer distances and to isolated regions, flights are common and can be cheaper than taking a bus. The bus and rail networks run frequent departures on almost every route, and timetables are never more than a few minutes out. A new, modern metro system has redefined getting around the country's largest city.

Before you leave

LAN's South America Airpass must be purchased before entering South America by someone residing outside the continent. It can be purchased directly through an LAN office, their website (*www.lan.com*) or through a travel agent. It is most economical if you arrive in Chile via LAN airlines.

Intercity travel

Air: Domestic air routes are extensive, even to small, backwater villages in Patagonia. The major domestic carrier is LAN, which flies many national and international routes, and Sky Airlines flies many of the same routes as LAN within the country for a fraction of the price. LAN has an Airpass, which can be used with international routes within the continent.

Boat: Some of the most exciting scenery can only be seen by boat – particularly the fiords and islands in Southern Patagonia. Several ferry

companies, such as Navimag and Transmarchilay, fill the routes, while many major cruise ships go around Cabo de Hornos and head up the Chilean coast. The longest trips may run no more than once a week during the summer months and far less at other times. Shorter trips to Chiloé and locations in Northern Patagonia not connected by road are more frequent.

Bus: Buses are comfortable and clean, offering meals and TV screens. Schedules are generally prompt and efficient, and seats are assigned. Rarely do they allow people to stand in the aisles. The largest carriers are Pullman and TurBus, which cover most of the country, while many smaller companies cover regional destinations. Outside of the summer season prices drop dramatically and reservations can be made just a few hours in advance.

A variety of classes exist. *Salón Cama* (sleeper) buses are the most expensive, have the best services and carry only 24 passengers. They cost 50 per cent more than regular buses. *Executivo* and *Semi-cama* have extra leg-room and calf rests, carrying just 38 passengers. The typical bus is the *Clásico*, which has 46 reclining seats.

Rail: The great Chilean rail system is still used while other networks in South America have fallen into ruin. Tracks are not extensive and run only in the centre and north, but they do cover several major routes to and from Santiago. Timetables can be found at the Empresa de Los Ferrocarriles del Estado website (*www.efe.cl*).

Driving

The PanAmerican Highway, or Route 5, extends parallel along the coast from the northern border with Peru to Quellón, Chiloé. Toll roads now divide the road into pieces and can be quite expensive if travelling long distances, particularly in the regions closest to Santiago. In general, Chile's network of roads is well maintained and markers are set every 5km (3 miles) on most roads. Speed limits range from 120km/h (75mph) on some highways to 50km/h (30mph) in cities.

In many cases, your own wheels are the only way to reach remote national parks. To hire a car you need to be 25, carry a major credit card and have a driver's licence from your home country. Sometimes an international driver's permit is required, although this depends on the agency. Car rental starts at about $40 per day for the smallest vehicle. Hertz (*Tel: 2-496-1111*), AVIS (*Tel: 600-601-9966*) and Budget (*Tel: 2-362-3200*) have offices in most major cities, tourist areas, and airports.

Local transport

Buses: Santiago is the only city with a tourist-friendly bus system. New, accordion-style buses have replaced most of the former diesel-eating combis. Tickets can be purchased from the driver. In smaller cities, large vans and small, often old buses run frequently to rural destinations.

Metros: An extensive, efficient and modern metro system now covers the entire Santiago metropolitan area and is used by almost one million people each day. A modern tram runs between Valparaíso and Viña del Mar as well, while electric trolleys roam parallel to the bay in Valparaíso. Single tickets can be bought in machines or windows in the stations. Prices vary between peak and non-peak times.

Taxis: Outside Santiago, most cities are small enough and the attractions central enough to make riding by taxi sufficient. Rates are quite reasonable, though rarely will a driver speak English, so try to have your destination written down. If the fare isn't metered, discuss the charge before getting in the cab. There is no tipping.

Accommodation

Chile has a complete range of accommodation that can fit any budget. Backpacker hostels and campsites cover the entire country, while isolated resorts in stunning natural settings are some of the finest in the world. As tourism to the country grows, so do the lodging options. Standards in general are much higher than in the rest of Latin America.

Outside of Santiago and major resort areas, hotels of comparable standards are significantly cheaper than in Europe or North America, although higher than elsewhere in Latin America. For instance, a clean yet basic mid-range hotel with hot water, cable TV, in a good location in a large city during the peak tourist season may run anywhere from $30–75. If you are in a small rural town, expect that price to drop about 25 per cent. Prices depend significantly on the season as well, particularly in Patagonia when there are few visitors during the low season and most hotels are underbooked. Rates may fall by as much as 50 per cent.

At most high-end hotels, a non-refundable 19 per cent IVA (value added tax) is added to the bill, although

Posada Río Serrano, a *refugio* in Parque Nacional Torres del Paine

Campsite near Parque Nacional Huerquehue

if you pay in US dollars you may be able to avoid the charge. Sometimes the tax is already included in the rates. Credit cards are accepted at most mid-range to high-end hotels, while hostels, B&Bs and budget accommodation generally insist on cash only.

Beach resorts

The north coast of the country enjoys a warm climate for much of the year, although the water, outside of Arica, tends to be cold due to the chilly Humboldt Current that runs along the coast. The beaches, however, are simply gorgeous. White sandy, palm-lined beaches stretch on for miles; many of them are absolutely deserted. In the summer major resort hotels around Viña del Mar, Iquique and La Serena are filled with visitors. A number of

those are quite exclusive and are as luxurious as a Caribbean resort with all the same amenities.

Cabins

Where there is camping, often there are *cabañas* (cabins). The small, basic rooms are excellent value for small groups, and usually include private bathrooms and a small kitchen. They are often found on the outskirts of resort towns or national parks, grouped in small villages.

Camping

Chile's national parks have some of the most well developed campgrounds in the world. In some places, such as Torres del Paine, they have clean toilet facilities and hot showers. Many also have laundry facilities, restaurants and *asado* (grill) areas. Prices are generally based on the site, rather than number of people. So if you are camping in a group you can get by relatively cheaply. Sernatur in Santiago has a free booklet listing nearly every campsite in the country (*see p29*). Camping equipment, although readily available all over the country, is quite expensive.

Casas de Familia

In the summer season, when many hotels are booked weeks or months in advance, many local families open up their home to travellers. *Casas de Familia* are usually a basic room with access to a communal bathroom. Many will offer breakfast as well. Generally the rooms are as comfortable as a low-end hotel or a hostal for well under the price. Often you will encounter someone waiting at the bus station with pictures of the rooms. Some indigenous

A B&B in Valparaíso

villages and farms have even started exchanging a room for labour. It's a great way to practise your Spanish and to get to know a local family. Most tourist offices keep lists of rooms for rent.

Hotels

The selection of hotels in the country is wide and growing rapidly. However, the country lacks a uniform rating system. Thus, in some instances many 1-star hotels may be better value than a 3-star. Many major North American chain hotels have touched down in Chilean cities as well, and the quality seems to be on par with the other locations. Most hotels include breakfast of some kind, be it basic continental with tea and a roll or a full buffet. Private bathrooms with hot water, cable TV and a telephone are quite normal even at the lower level hotels. Reservations in the high season should be made weeks or months ahead.

Luxury hotels

Many upscale hotels, aimed at the growing number of business travellers, are making their way to the country. Most have large pools, fitness rooms, access to golf courses (which are all private in the country) and world-class restaurants and shops. The first Ritz Carlton in South America opened up a branch in Santiago and is considered to be one of the finest hotels on the continent. Rooms start at around $200 a night for a standard twin.

Refugios

Refugios (nature lodges) are an important aspect of travel in Chile and often the most memorable experience of one's trip to the country. These hotels are set amid some of the country's most beautiful scenery, occasionally in the middle of isolated parks, and offer a range of amenities. Many are basic, with communal rooms and baths and a small restaurant. Others, however, employ world-class chefs and are frequented by some of the wealthiest people in the world. The Explora Hotels in Torres del Paine and San Pedro de Atacama are considered to be some of the world's most luxurious and may charge as much as $500 a night.

Spas

With so many thermal springs in the country, it's no shock that many spas take advantage of the curative hot waters. Many are set in the Lakes District and Northern Patagonia, and combine full spa amenities such as massages, body treatments and yoga classes. The best will have a variety of clean, modern pools at different temperatures. Prices range considerably, from $50 a night in a basic cabin to $1,000 for a five-night package with meals and treatments.

Telos

As most unmarried people still live with their parents, many Chileans may dip into one of these small

Beach condos at Playa Cavancha, La Serena

'love hotels' that charge for just hours at a time.

Youth hostels

These are generally the lowest priced accommodation option in any city. Most are clean and comfortable and filled with young, international travellers on a lengthy trip. Most often rooms and bathrooms are shared and they may include breakfast and amenities such as TV lounges, kitchen use, free internet connection, international phone calls, tourist information and money exchange. Non-HI (Hostelling International) members may be charged a slight increase in fee. However, cards are not required. Asociación Chilena de Albergues Turísticos Juveniles in Santiago (*Tel: 2-233-3220. www.hostelling.cl*) is the national affiliate of HI and sells memberships.

Food and drink

With one of the most diverse landscapes on the planet, it is only natural that Chileans have an array of dishes. Food varies greatly from the interior to the coast. Seafood, some of the best in the world, varies from region to region, while mouthwatering Chilean beef can be found everywhere. Places like Chiloé have their own unique cuisines, while the Lakes District has myriad recipes and beers influenced by German settlers.

Meals

Small meals are typical in Chile. It is usual to have three or four meals a day. *Desayuno* (breakfast) is fairly light and usually nothing more than a roll with butter and jam with coffee or tea. In some places you may find it includes eggs, or thin slices of ham and cheese. *Almuerzo* (lunch) is the largest meal of the day, normally taken between 1–2.30pm. *Onces* (elevenses) are afternoon tea taken around 5pm.

Mussels and *piures*, a local shellfish, drying in Angelmó

Cena (dinner) is generally very light and may consist of just a sandwich or *empanada* (snack).

Ceviche

Ceviche is raw fish marinated in lime. Technically it isn't raw like sushi, as the acid in the lime cooks the fish as you eat it. In much of the country it is quite bland and served with just a few herbs, but in the north they tend to spice it up quite a bit.

Chilean beef

North American and European visitors will find the quality of red meat served here far exceeds that to which they are accustomed. A *parilladas* is a mix of grilled meat such as steak, chicken, pork and chorizo. *Chorilliana* is a plate of French fries piled with fried steak, potatoes, grilled onions and a fried egg. *Lomo á la Pobre*, poor man's steak, is a large cut of beef topped with a fried egg and fries. *Cordero* is lamb, known best in Southern Patagonia where it is spit-roasted over an open fire. *Chirqui* is dried meat, usually alpaca, and most often found in the Altiplano.

Curanto

Curanto – one of the more interesting seafood preparations – originated in Chiloé. Shellfish, fish, meat, potatoes and vegetables covered in *gunnera* leaves, are cooked in a hole in the earth that is filled with red hot stones. The idea is to have a mix that is a little bit of everything. Many believe that the

preparation shows a direct link between South America and Polynesia, as many islands in the South Pacific prepare dishes using the same method.

Empanadas

Empanadas are snack-sized turnovers filled with meat, cheese or shellfish, and are a staple of Chilean food. They can be made *al horno* (baked) or *frito* (fried). *Empanadas* are found absolutely everywhere, from a small stand in the street, a roving vendor with a small basket on a bus, to an upscale bakery in a chic Santiago neighbourhood.

Seafood

Chile's seafood is the shining star of its dining scene. The quality and variety is unequalled anywhere in the world. There is a long list of fish and shellfish: mussels, clams, urchins, oysters, scallops, salmon, sea bass and sea cucumbers. Visit any coastal fish market in the morning for an overwhelming assault on your senses. There are a number of preparations that originate from pre-Colombian times. *Caldillos* are fish stews with potatoes, onions and carrots. *Caldillo de Congrio* (conger eel) is one of the most popular. *Paila marina*, a favourite of Pablo Neruda, is a shellfish stew available throughout the country.

Sandwiches and *completos*

Junk food served from street stalls and in 1950s-style American diners is popular in much of the country,

Food and drink

Salteado de Mariscos, a Peruvian dish popular in the Norte Grande

particularly in the evening and after a long night out. *Completos* are basic hot dogs slathered in mayo, avocado and a number of other condiments. The *barros jarpa* is a toasted sandwich of ham and melted cheese. Other sandwiches include the *barros luco* (steak and melted cheese) and *churrasco palta* (grilled beef and avocado).

Desserts

Europe's culinary influence can best be seen in the country's desserts. *Helados* (ice cream) – usually Italian-style – is everywhere in many flavours, including national ones such as *lucuma*, a creamy fruit endemic to Chile and Peru. *Dulce de leche*, also known as *manjar blanco*, is a creamy filling made of milk and sugar and is used in many pastries. *Churros* are fried doughnut-like treats filled with anything from chocolate to *manjar blanco*. *Sopapillas* are fried dough sweetened with honey, often found being fried right in the street. *Kuchen*, German tarts, cakes and pastries, are found throughout the Lakes District.

Maté

Maté is actually a drink from Uruguay but popular in both Argentina and Chile. It uses *yerba maté*, a type of grassy, bitter tea made from a South American species of holly, which is drunk from a small gourd with a metal spoon called a *bombilla*. Drinking *maté* is a very common social practice in Chile.

Pisco

(*see page 57*)

Wine

(*see pages 72–3*)

Entertainment

Chileans love to let loose and are always ready to have a good time. Santiago has one of the most diverse entertainment and nightlife options of any large city in Latin America, from a robust theatre and classical music selections to a hip and contemporary nightlife, where the dancing continues until dawn. The best international rock bands always make the capital a stop on their world tours. Elsewhere the trend continues with laid-back restobars, traditional music venues and lively folk festivals.

Clubs, discos, live houses and bars

With some of the best beer and wine in Latin America and the world's most comprehensive Pisco culture, nights out are a big part of society, from refined drinking dens to discos that stay open until the early hours.

Cinema

The film industry took a hit during the Pinochet years, as freedom of expression was somewhat limited, but has rebounded and many of the old classics from Chilean and exiled directors, such as Patricio Guzmán and Raúl Ruiz and Silvio Caiozzi, are becoming popular once again. Current Hollywood films are shown most often with Spanish subtitles, although they are at times translated. See listings in any city's daily newspaper for times.

Information

Most cities with active nightlife and entertainment cultures have a number of free information booklets and newspapers, often in both Spanish and English, providing entertainment listings in detail. In Santiago, Valparaíso and Viña del Mar, try *El Mercurio* newspaper. Pick up a copy of *Rocinante* magazine for the best arts listings. The English language *Santiago Times* is a good place to search for events catering for the expat community. A number of small, frequently coming and going tourist info booklets and guides can be found in shops, cafés and restaurants in most major tourist areas.

Reservations

Make reservations through your hotel or buy tickets through Teleticket (*www.teleticket.cl*), a booth located in most supermarkets and department stores.

Sign at Santiago theatre

Shopping

Chile has the complete range of shopping experiences. There are high-end boutiques with the world's most chic designer labels found by the dozen, while unusual artisan markets filled with beautifully made indigenous handicrafts can't be found anywhere else. Quality is good all around. But it isn't just new items that will catch your attention. Perhaps inspired by the bric-a-brac in poet Pablo Neruda's houses, antiques and collectibles are everywhere; often right in the street. It's a collector's dream come true.

Although you may have many of the same stores, most of the products are significantly higher priced in Chile. Adventure gear from top brands such as North Face can be found across the country, as many are stocking up before a big hike, climb or adventure. The selection is often better than other countries, with many outfitters selling numerous brands sitting side by side and lining the major streets in places

such as Pucón, Punta Arenas and Puerto Natales. High-end fashion labels such as Chanel or Louis Vuitton tend to be priced more or less the same as elsewhere. Most shops open Monday–Friday 9am–8pm and Saturday 9am–2pm. Sunday openings are rare but do occur in some places. Shopping malls and department stores are open daily from 10am–9pm. Many small, independent shops may close for lunch in the middle of the day.

Shopping centres and department stores

Chile is proud of its shopping centres and department stores, which are as big and brash as those in Europe or North America. Most have a combination of international chain stores and restaurants mixed with national and Latin American ones. A number of large department store chains can be found in every major city. Falabella, Almacenes Paris and Ripley are Chile's

Vegetables for sale at Temuco market

three largest and sell just about everything, including brand name clothing, electronics, house wares, sportswear and accessories.

Tax-free shopping

Chile has an incredibly high sales tax that averages about 18 per cent. The Zona Francas or duty free zones in several regions on the extreme ends of the country get around this tax. Such outlets are like huge shopping centres selling just about any item that is imported to Chile. They exist in Punta Arenas and the entire region of Tarapaca (centering in Iquique), and are great spots to buy large items such as TVs and cars, as well as clothing, cameras and MP3 players.

What to buy

Antiques

Chile has numerous antique markets in streets and parks of many cities on certain days of the week. If you like what you see in Pablo Neruda's houses, chances are you can find it in the street in Valparaíso, Santiago or Arica.

Handicrafts

Mapuche woollen goods, basketry, carvings and jewellery based on traditional design are of high quality and make excellent gifts and can be found all across the La Araucanía. The Aymara weave some fine Alapaca scarves and sweaters, the selection may not be as wide as in Peru or Bolivia, but the price and basic quality is generally

North Face store in Punta Arenas

just as good. With silver being a major export, many artisans have turned to jewellery making. Prices are often significantly cheaper for rings and necklaces made of silver than in Europe or North America. Non-jewellery items such as candleholders, silverware and figurines can be found as well.

Lapis lazuli

This rare blue stone, found only in Chile or Afghanistan, is a great buy for jewellery. Every major jewellery shop has some design with lapis lazuli. Artisan markets throughout the country have relatively affordable pieces, although the quality is not always as good. The best selection of pieces can be found in the Bellavista district of Santiago. (*See pp146–7.*)

Woollen items

In Chiloé and Patagonia, inexpensive and high quality woollen goods can be found on markets and in craft shops. The sweaters, scarves and blankets make excellent souvenirs.

Lapis lazuli

The extremely rare stone called lapis lazuli has been a favourite of pharaohs and kings for thousands of years, but it was only during the last hundred years that it was found in Chile. The Chilean lapis lazuli mine, called Flor de los Andes, sits in the 3,600m (11,811ft) mountains of Ovalle. The mine only opened in the late 19th century, and it wasn't until 1950 that the bluest stones began to be extracted and appeared on the retail market.

Lapis lazuli jewellery

The light or dark blue lapis lazuli stones only exist in Chile, while the much lighter, almost violet-coloured, stone can be found in the Badakshan area of Afghanistan, which has been continually mined since ancient times. Afghanistan is the only other country to have a significant deposit of the blue stone. Small deposits have also been found in Canada, the US, Mongolia, Italy and Burma.

The stone is very rare and has been classed as a highly precious stone since ancient times, when it was thought to have magical powers. The Egyptians were highly fond of this stone and used it for amulets and scarabs. In fact, it has been found in burial sights dating back 5,000 years. Cleopatra often wore it, and the death mask of Tutankhamun combined it with gold. Egyptian women also used a powder form of the stone as an eye shadow.

The Romans thought it was an aphrodisiac, while in the Middle Ages it was thought to protect people from disease and keep the soul clean. Many of the world's most beloved paintings used the ground-up stone for blue paint, although a synthetic colour was developed in 1834.

Lapis lazuli jewellery display

Today, it is regarded as the stone of friendship and truth and thought to encourage harmony in relationships.

The opaque rock consists mainly of diopside and lazurite and is formed during the metamorphosis of lime to marble over millions of years. The gold specks found within the stone are generally understood to show the authenticity and increase the value. Since magnification cannot show the quality of the stone, the quality is judged by properties such as scarcity, stability and colour. By these standards there are no first-, second- or third-quality stones.

In Chile, lapis lazuli can be found in gift shops and jewellers throughout the country and is one of the primary gifts any tourist brings back on a trip to the country. Necklaces, earrings, bracelets, cufflinks, pendants, candleholders and silverware are adorned with it here and many shops have significant sections of their store dedicated to the stone. To help preserve it from everyday wear, a good tip is to protect it from acidic substances and avoid exposure to too much sunlight. Taking it to a jeweller to have it repolished from time to time will help to revive the colour of the stone. The best shops can be found in the Bellavista neighbourhood of Santiago, which crowd the corner of Av Bellavista and Pio Nono.

Sport and leisure

Chile may be one of the world's leaders in extreme and adventure sports, but organised sports are enjoyed by many. Several are regionally focused, such as the cowboy-like rodeo huasa in the north and central regions, while skiing, fútbol and a number of other sports can be found all over the country. There are even a few indigenous games that have been kept alive and are still played frequently today.

Chueca

This traditional Mapuche team game means 'curved stick' and was once played between rival groups in order to avoid armed conflict. The game starts in a central hole and teams try to hit a ball with the *chueca* to the opposite end of the field where a line is drawn and they receive a point. The game is over when there are five points (although this sometimes changes) and lasts for hours. The game was developed long before the Spaniards arrived and can be quite brutal. After the game there is a celebration with heavy drinking of *chichi*, prayers, dancing and feasting, which is meant to fortify communal relationships. The game is difficult to encounter and rarely scheduled, although if you happen to encounter a Mapuche village on the right day, you may find a game in progress.

Fitness

Chile's middle classes are caught up in the fitness craze as much as anywhere in North America or Europe. Most hotels now provide fitness facilities and large cities have state-of-the-art gyms as well.

Football

The number one sport in the country is without a doubt *fútbol* (soccer). Many consider it Chile's national sport and major games such as championships and World Cup qualifiers attract as many as 80,000 people to Santiago's National Stadium. The best teams include Colo Colo, Universidad Católica and Universidad de Chile, all based in Santiago.

Golf

Chile boasts 58 clubs, including one in Punta Arenas, which is the southernmost golf club in the world. The sport dates back from the second half of the 19th century when a group of expat Englishmen founded the Playa Ancha Golf Club in Valparaíso. All courses are private and in order to play you must be a registered guest at certain hotels or go with a member. Green fees run at about US$70 for 18 holes.

Horse racing

Horse racing, which attracts a large number of gamblers to the tracks surrounding Santiago, is similar to any other country. Tracks are lively, minimum bets are US$0.35, entry is just $1, and it's a great way to waste an afternoon and see Santiaguinos letting loose.

Rayuela

This Chilean game involves throwing heavy metal disks called *tejos* (children may use coins) in the hope of landing on a string that is stretched across a yard. It's played mostly by men, often in teams and in rural areas.

Rodeo

Also called the *huasa*, the Chilean rodeo is a bit different from those in North America and a whole subculture has developed around it. The *Huasos*, or Chilean cowboys, dress in colourful ponchos, fringed leggings, flat-topped hats, high-heeled boots and large spurs. In the competitions, which take place in arenas called *media lunas* (half moons), a two-man team attempts to control a steer by making it stop in a certain place without using a lasso. Rodeo teams travel from village to village taking part in different events during the autumn, with the finals held in Rancagua in late March/early April.

Skiing

(*See pp82–3.*)

Surfing

(*See pp150–51.*)

Kayaks in Coyhaique, Northern Patagonia

An adventurer's paradise

Surrounded by stunning natural beauty and one of the most diverse topographies of any country in the world, it is no wonder that Chile is a haven for sports enthusiasts. The Andes Mountains create numerous activities for hiking through immaculate mountain panoramas filled with glaciers and rafting over raging rivers, culminating in the south at Parque Nacional Torres del Paine, the country's crown jewel.

Many of the paramount activities take place in the southern half of the country. Parque Nacional Torres del Paine in Southern Patagonia is one of the most sought after **hiking** destinations in the world. The four- to five-day 'W' trek, as well as the longer circuits, are completed by thousands each year. Elsewhere, remarkable trails can be found further south on Isla Navarino or in the national parks that line the Andes south of Santiago. The creation of the Sendero de Chile (*www.senderodechile.cl*), a major project linking the entire country from north to south by hiking trails, is

Kayaking in Río Serrano in Torres del Paine National Park

Rowing in Lago Villarica

underway. It is perhaps the most ambitious trail network in the world today. Only small sections are open, including trails on Easter Island.

Similarly, **climbing** on a number of the tallest peaks in South America – some of them active volcanoes – can be attempted. A range of technical expertise is necessary; however, several of the peaks can be climbed in under a day by those without any mountaineering expertise, such as Volcán Villarica near Pucón.

For **rafting**, the Futaleufú is one of the finest whitewater rivers in the world, with aqua blue water intersecting large boulders and snow-covered mountains. The rapids range from Class IV to V+ during the peak season. Hydroelectricity projects have dammed some of the best rafting rivers, but many other challenging spots still exist, such as on the Ríos

Baker and Simpson. **Kayaking** is a great alternative way to see a number of the fiords and bays of several parks, from Pumalín and Chiloé, and some visitors even make their way around Cabo de Hornos this way.

Mountain Biking trails are numerous, with the Andes offering various climbs and descents for a range of skill levels. Biking the Carretera Austral – one of the most scenic roadways in the world – has become a bragging point among the country's best cyclists, although the route can only be attempted during the summer months.

Although the green hills and forests are rare, the north of Chile offers a range of activities not found elsewhere in the country. In Iquique, the strong wind currents that rise off the coastal cliffs attract numerous **paragliders** each day, with glides possible for dozens or even hundreds of kilometres. The nearby dunes have taken up a sport that is only attempted in nearby Peru and a few Middle Eastern countries: **sandboarding**. Like snowboarding, thrill seekers race down the beaches on boards, but from the top of a sandy dune. **Surfing** is the most attempted sport in the north, however, with the warm waters of Arica being the epicentre and home to the annual national championships.

Children

Children's entertainment is a new concept in Latin America, but Chile is leading the way. The country is a very family-friendly place and many locations in the country are sure to have a number of activities that kids will love. Where there are extreme adventure sports for the world's best athletes, there will be tamer versions for children. Museums in many parts of the country, particularly Santiago, are highly interactive and many are aimed solely at children. Perhaps the best amusement park on the continent is here, as well as many national parks filled with scores of rare and interesting animals.

Santiago
Fantasilandia
This is Chile's largest amusement park and has numerous modern roller coasters and rides, as well as carnival games. It's not as good as top theme parks in North America or Europe, but will nevertheless keep the kids entertained.
Av Beaucheff 938. Tel: 2-476-8600. Open: Tue–Fri 11am–8pm, Sat–Sun 2am–8pm. Admission charge. Metro: Parque O'Higgins.

Gran Circo Teatro
Circus troupe and experimental theatre that's great for kids and adults.
Av Vicuña Mackenna 37, Lastarria. Tel: 2-222-1530. Metro: Baquedano.

Museo de Ciencia y Tecnología
Science museum with interactive activities relating to astronomy, geology and history.
Quinta Normal. Tel: 2-681-6022. Open: Tue–Fri 10am–6pm, Sat–Sun 11am–6pm. Admission charge. Metro: Quinta Normal.

Museo Interactivo Mirador
One of the country's best places that's oriented towards children. This interactive museum includes art and craft workshops, music rooms, funny mirrors and numerous exhibits relating to Chile's history.
Punta Arenas 6711. Tel: 2-280-7800. Open: Mon 9.30am–1.30pm, Tue–Sun 9.30am–6.30pm. Admission charge. Metro: Mirador.

Parque Metropolitano
Cerro San Cristóbal, a mountain overlooking the centre of the city, is mostly covered by this park complex. There's a small zoo at the midway point and several swimming pools, lookout telescopes, ice cream stands and of

course, beautiful views. It is reached by a Teleferiqo or funicular railway, which climbs the steep mountainsides.

Funicular: Open: Mon 1–8pm, Tue–Sun 10am–8pm. Admission charge.
Teleferiqo: Open: Mon 2.30–6.30pm, Tue–Fri noon–6.30pm, Sat–Sun 10.30am–7.30pm. Admission charge.

Pucón
Race park
Minibikes and go-carts race around a circular dirt track.
Av Colo-Colo and Av O'Higgins. Admission charge.

Beaches
The north coast of the country is lined with white sand Pacific beaches that are extremely family friendly, particularly during the summer months. Pony rides, water sports, beach games and ice cream are offered every 5m (16ft). The beaches around Viña del Mar, La Serena, Arica and Iquique are the most developed.

Ski resorts
Considering that most of Chile's ski resorts are family oriented, most have numerous activities for children. Most resorts have indoor pools, games rooms, ice skating rinks, ski camps and races. Special deals often allow kids to ski free for a week or have free ski lessons at certain times of the year. There are also bunny slopes for inexperienced skiers. Portillo is especially child-friendly.

A clown in Valparaíso keeps the children amused

Essentials

Arriving

Almost all international flights land in Santiago, with many departures throughout the day from the US and Europe, and just one daily flight from Australia and Tahiti. Most regional routes leave just once or twice a day.

Entry formalities

Tourists from North America and Europe are generally granted 90-day tourist visas upon arrival. Reciprocal visa fees are issued to US ($100), Canadian ($55) and Australian ($30) citizens upon arrival by air, although not overland. It is a one-time fee that extends for the life of the passport.

By air

There are direct flights from the US, Europe, New Zealand, Tahiti and many Latin American destinations. Nearly all international flights land and depart at Santiago's Aeropuerto Internacional Arturo Merino Benítez, also called Pudahuel. The national carrier is LAN airlines, which has the most international and interior flights to and in the country. Some flights from Argentina land in Puerto Montt's Aeropuerto Carlos Ibáñez del Campo.

To and from Pudahuel

The airport is 26km (16 miles) west of the centre. If you have hotel reservations, most will arrange a pick up. The easiest way to the centre is to catch the **Centropuerto** bus that runs to and from the La Moneda metro station or the Pajaritos metro station. **Taxis** to and from the airport are quite reasonably priced as well, ranging between $15–20. Tickets for communal **minibuses** (Transvip, Delfos and other companies) can be bought in the arrivals hall and prices are just $6–8 per person direct to your hotel.

Customs

Individual travellers may import the following items duty free: 400 cigarettes, 50 cigars or 500 grams of tobacco, 2.5l of alcohol and perfume for personal use. By taking illegal drugs into or out of the country you risk severe incurring penalties; if you are carrying prescription medication, be sure to take a letter from your doctor.

Communications
Public phones

Public phones are tricky and expensive to use. One hundred pesos will last just a minute and even less for a call to a mobile phone. Some phones will only take coins; other phones will take only calling cards, and other phones won't take either. Your best bet when calling any number is to go to a call centre that has a number of booths for a much more reasonable price.

International calls

Centros de llamadas (call centres) can be found in even the smallest towns where you can walk into a booth and dial anywhere in the world. Sometimes you will have to give the number to the clerk who will dial the number and point you to a booth when/if it is answered. Other times you can simply dial the number from a booth. Often there will be a meter beside the phone, which will keep tabs on what the call is costing. Otherwise, look for a list of minute charges for different destinations, which should be posted nearby. Rates to the US and Europe tend to be the same as if calling another Latin American country. In general, calls to mobile phones tend to be more than double those to a landline phone. All non-local calls will need area and country codes to be dialled.

Mobile phones

If you plan on spending an extended period of time in Chile, a mobile phone may be a convenient option. Prepaid phones, where you can buy a phone and then charge up, are popular. You can also bring a sim-unlocked GSM-compatible phone (1900MHZ frequency) and simply buy a sim card from any Chilean mobile company, such as Telefonica or Entel.

Internet

Staying in touch by email is an excellent option. There are many cyber cafés in every city that charge by the hour or minute, usually no more than one dollar per hour. Having an account with a POP server such as Yahoo, Hotmail or Gmail is easiest, as you can access it from anywhere. The computers generally are more up-to-date than other Latin American countries and often high speed; although in some rural areas they may be extremely slow. Many are equipped with CD writers, cameras and headsets.

Useful numbers
Directory Assistance: *103*
Entel: *800-360-066*
Telefonica: *800-800-044*

Electricity

Electrical plugs in Chile look like two round pins. They run at 220 volts, alternating at 50 cycles per second. Most visitors will need a voltage converter – these are availiable in the airport or from any electronics or

REGIONAL TELEPHONE CODES

Antofagasta	55	Recreo	32
Arica	58	San Bernardo	2
Calama	56	Santiago	2
Chiguayante	41	Talca	71
Concepción	41	Talcahuano	41
Iquique	57	Temuco	45
La Serena	51	Valparaíso	32
Penco	41	Viña del Mar	32
Rancagua	72		

hardware store. Combination adapters, which adjust to any worldwide voltage system, can also be found.

Media

There is a wide range of tourist-related English media available, although for news you are limited to the online only *Santiago Times* (*www.tcgnews.com/santiagotimes*). The conservative *El Mercurio* is Santiago's largest newspaper, although read almost exclusively by the upper classes. You can find English-language newspapers at newsstands in the centre and Providencia, although usually they are several days behind. Many television programmes are in English with Spanish subtitles, while many North American channels in Spanish can be heard in English by using the SAP button on the remote control. News channels such as CNN and the BBC are on every cable network.

Money

The national currency is the Chilean peso and is broken into denominations of 500, 1,000, 2,000, 5,000, 10,000 and 20,000 peso notes and 1, 5, 10, 50, 100 and 500 peso coins. Euros, pounds and most other currencies can only be exchanged in *Casas de Cambio* in large cities or tourist areas, while the US dollar can be exchanged nearly everywhere. Many large hotels, tourist

Beaver hides on sale in Porvenir

agencies and restaurants will accept US dollars. Exchange rates tend to be best in Santiago. ATMs are everywhere and give good exchange rates, but will charge anywhere from $1–5 for a withdrawal, depending on your bank. Credit cards are accepted almost everywhere, although some businesses charge up to 6 per cent extra to cover the transaction. Traveller's cheques are rarely used here and exchange rates are very poor.

National holidays

On public holidays, many stores and all public offices close for the day. Public transport is operable in some instances; however, the schedule is limited.

1 January – Año Nuevo
(New Year's Day)
March or April – Semana Santa
(Easter Week)
1 May – Día del Trabajo
(Labour Day)
21 May – Glorias Navles
(commemoration of the naval battle of Iquique)
30 May – Corpus Christi
29 June – Día de San Pedro
y San Pablo (St Peter & St Paul's Day)
15 August – Asunción de la Virgen
(Assumption)
18 September – Día de la
Independencia Nacional
(National Independence Day)
19 September – Día de Ejército
(Armed Forces Day)
12 October – Día de la Raza
(Columbus Day)

1 November – Todo los Santos
(All Saints' Day)
8 December – Inmaculada Concepción
(Immaculate Conception)
25 December – Navidad
(Christmas Day)

Opening hours

Most banks open Monday–Friday 9am–2pm, while most ATMs operate 24 hours. Most shops and supermarkets are open Monday–Friday 9am–8pm and Saturday 9am–2pm. Most shopping centres are open daily from 10am–9pm. Bars and clubs open from 7pm or later and close between 4 and 5am. Many museums close on Mondays.

Post offices

Correos de Chile, the national post office, was privatised in 2002. Most post offices are open Monday–Friday 9am–5pm and Saturday 9am–noon. Letters take about two weeks to reach the US or Europe. Important overseas mail should be sent *certifacado* (certified). Often packages must be inspected by a customs official before being brought to the post office. Vendors will package parcels for a small fee and are usually stationed just outside post offices. *Poste restante* (to be collected) packages are often thrown out after being held for more than 30 days.

Suggested reading

Birds of Chile (Princeton Field Guides) by Alvaro Jaramillo, Peter Burke and David Beadle (2003)

Chile: The Other September 11: An Anthology of Reflections on the 1973 Coup (Radical History) by Ariel Dorfman, Pilar Aguilera and Ricardo Fredes (2006)

Five Decades: Poems 1925–1970 (Neruda, Pablo) by Pablo Neruda and Ben Belitt (1994)

In Patagonia by Bruce Chatwin (1977)

My Invented Country: A Nostalgic Journey Through Chile by Isabel Allende (2003)

Selected Poems of Gabriela Mistral (Mary Burritt Christiansen Poetry Series) by V B Price and Ursula K Le Guin (2003)

Travels in a Thin Country: A Journey Through Chile (Modern Library (Paperback)) by Sara Wheeler (1999)

The Wines of Chile (Classic Wine Library) by Peter Richards (2006)

Tax

Chile imposes a VAT or Impuesto al Valor Agregado (IVA) of 18 per cent on most goods and services.

Time differences

Chile is four hours behind Greenwich Mean Time for most of the year. During daylight savings time, usually between mid-December and late March, the country is only three hours behind.

Tipping

Outside the top restaurants, large cities and tourist areas, tipping hasn't really caught on in Chile. With the exception of small, family-run restaurants, a 10 per cent tip is expected. In taxis and cafés, simply rounding up your bill is considered generous, although not expected.

Toilets

Chilean toilets look just like Western toilets, but paper products are never flushed. Usually there is a small dustbin with a lid where toilet tissues are disposed. Major hotels that have installed their own septic systems may overcome this issue.

Tourist offices

The Servicio Nacional de Turismo (Sernatur) is quite convenient and has offices all over the country. Their website (*www.sernatur.cl*) has loads of information about travelling in the country and a tourist hotline (*600-7376-2887*) is there for whenever you have any questions. Offices are usually filled with knowledgeable and multi-lingual staff who are more than happy to help with any questions. They can provide a number of basic, yet good, maps and brochures on any region or city in Chile. Often they will have information in English as well.

The national office is in **Santiago** *Av Providencia 1550, piso 2, Providencia. Tel: 2-731-8419.*

Regional and municipal tourist offices can provide more specific details on particular areas, although the quality of the information and services vary greatly. Offices are most often found on the main square or in bus terminals.

Municipalidad de Santiago *Oficina de Turismo Cerro Santo Lucia, Terraza Neptuno, Centro. Tel: 2-415-0667.*

Travellers with disabilities

Facilities for travellers with a disability are among the best in Latin America, although not nearly as good as in Western countries. Many luxury hotels are equipped to accommodate visitors with a disability and wheelchairs, but this is rare outside the capital. Linea 5 of Santiago's metro is wheelchair-accessible, as are several other random metro stations. Often entrance fees to national parks and tours are discounted for travellers with a disability, and Navimag ferries may give a free upgrade. **Tixi Service** (*Tel: 800-372-300, www.tixi.cl*) is a wheelchair-accommodating transport service in Santiago.

Water

Tap water is safe in most cities, although in the north bottled water is recommended.

Websites

There are many bilingual websites focused on national (*www.sernatur.cl, www.chile.com, www.visit-chile.org, www.turismochile.com*) and regional (*www.rutadelvino.cl, www.regionloslagos.cl, www.patagonia-chile.com*) tourist destinations. Other good sites include Suite 101's South America Travel page (*http://southamericatravel.suite101.com*), which has frequent articles and blogs on travel in South America, while the South American Explorers' web page (*www.saexpolorers.org*) has loads of information on every south American country, including trip reports by members accessible if you are a member.

Palacio de la Moneda, Santiago

Language

Although Spanish speakers in Latin America and Spain generally understand each other, there are some differences in the language. These can be compared to the differences in British English and American English. First of all, Spanish is often referred to as Castellano in Chile and other Latin American countries. One of the main differences is that many Spaniards often pronounce the *z* and the *c* before *i* or *e* like the 'th' in 'thin', while many Latin Americans pronounce it the same as the s. Outside Argentina, Latin American countries do not use the '*vosotros*' verb form, rather they prefer '*ustedes*'.

Many say the Chileans don't speak Spanish. They speak Chileno, as the accent and pronunciation of many words is often difficult to comprehend, even by native Spanish speakers. Some words have been imported from Mapudungun, Quechua and German, and many are highly regional. Speakers use large amounts of slang as well.

Spanish pronunciation by Chileans may be difficult to understand at first. They often leave out end consonants. For instance '*va*mos', or '*let's go*', sounds more like '*vamo*', as the 's' seemingly disappears. Similarly with the word '*islas*', sounds like '*ila*', and '*buenos días*' sounds like '*bueno día*'.

There are also many words or expressions used solely in Chile, nicknamed Chilenisms, that you won't find in any dictionary. Often they won't mean anything outside the country. Instead of '*Cómo estas?*' or 'How are you?', Chileans may say '*Cómo estai?*' The word '*pues*', similar to an English 'well', is shortened to '*pue*' or '*po*'. *Huevón* is the favourite Chilean swear word, and can be used as a put-down or a term of endearment, depending on the situation.

Titles: Always use titles such as *Señor* or *Señora* until you get to know someone, particularly an older person. Chileans tend to be quite formal in most instances.

Imported words: You will be surprised at how many cognates or imported words come from English. Often you can hispinicise an English word to be understood.

Basic words and phrases

Good morning	*Buenos días*
Good afternoon	*Buenas tardes*
Good evening/night	*Buenas noches*
How are you?	*¿Cómo estas?*
Yes, please	*Sí, por favor*
No, thank you	*No, gracias*
Please	*Por favor*
Please give me	*Por favor, deme…*
Yes, just a little	*Si, un poco*
No, I can't	*No, no puedo*
Thanks/Thank you	*Gracias*
Thank you very much	*Muchas gracias*
Goodbye	*Adiós*
Sorry, excuse me	*Perdón, disculpe*
Sorry	*Perdón*
Excuse me	*Disculpe*
Excuse me, do you speak English?	*¿Disculpe usted habla inglés?*
I don't understand	*No entiendo/ No comprendo*
Please take me to	*Por favor lléveme a/hacia*
How much will it cost to go to	*¿Cuánto cuesta ir a….?*
It's an emergency	*Es una emergencia*
I'm lost	*Estoy perdido/a*
Today	*Hoy*
Tomorrow	*Mañana*
Yesterday	*Ayer*
Tonight	*Esta noche*

Numbers

1	*uno*	**7**	*siete*
2	*dos*	**8**	*ocho*
3	*tres*	**9**	*nueve*
4	*cuatro*	**10**	*diez*
5	*cinco*	**100**	*cien*
6	*seis*	**1,000**	*mil*

These are combined to make larger numbers: e.g.

18 (*diez y ocho*), **23** (*veinte y tres*), **142** (*cientocuarenta y dos*) and so on.

Emergencies

Help!	*Auxilio! Ayuda!*
Watch out!	*Cuidado!*
It hurts!	*Me duele!*
I feel ill	*Me siento mal/ Me siento enfermo*

Directions

Straight ahead	*Siga de frente*
Right	*Derecha*
Left	*Izquierda*
Stop here	*Pare aquí*
I want to go to	*Deseo ir a…./ Quiero ir a…*

Emergencies

Emergency numbers
Police: *133*
Fire: *132*
Ambulance: *131*
Directory assistance: *103*

Health, safety and crime
Crime
Chile is one of the safest countries in Latin America. However, robberies do still occur. In Santiago, Valparaíso and other large cities in particular, precautions should be made. Keep a close eye on your belongings and your wallet in central plazas and at bus and train terminals. Most crime is petty; violent crime is quite rare even in Santiago. Theft on beaches is fairly common, so you should never leave your valuables unattended.

Health
Food-borne illnesses are common to many Western travellers and are the biggest general threat. Be careful particularly in small, rural restaurants and with street food, making sure that everything is thoroughly cooked. *Ceviche* (raw fish marinated in lime) poses some risk if it is not properly prepared, although ill effects are quite rare. As Chile lies in a mostly temperate zone, mosquito-borne illnesses are extremely rare.

Altitude sickness is common in the Andes, particularly in the Altiplano in Parque Nacional Lauca and on hikes and climbs to the highest peaks. Sorojche pills, available at any pharmacy, are taken to ease the effects, while coca tea is a common, although not medically proven, treatment. The best cure, however, is moving to lower altitudes.

Be sure to take out travel insurance to cover health (*see opposite*): Chile has some of the best medical facilities in Latin America and many are similar to those in North America or Europe. Prices are a little bit lower as well.

Major hotels carry lists of English-speaking staff at hospitals and medical clinics. In Santiago try:

Clínica Alemana *Av Vitacura 5951, Vitacura. Tel: 2-212-9700.*

Clínica Las Condes *Lo Fonticella 441, Las Condes. Tel: 2-210-4000.*

Pharmacies
Chilean pharmacies are well stocked with many American and European medicines, vitamins and cosmetics. Vitamins and cosmetics tend to be far more expensive, while many pharmaceuticals are cheaper or similarly priced. Many pharmacies are open 24 hours.

Farmacia Ahumada (*tel: 2-222-4000*) is the best and largest chain of chemists and has branches all over the country, including dozens in Santiago. They will deliver orders to your hotel or residence for a small fee. Hospitals also supply drugs.

Embassies and consulates

Nearly all embassies and consulates are found in Santiago, although several consulates for neighbouring countries can be found in major border cities.

For countries other than those listed, check the Yellow Pages telephone directory (*www.yell.com*), or visit *www.paginasamarillas.cl*

Australia
Isidora Goyenechea 3621, 13th Floor, Las Condes. Tel: 2-550-3500.
www.chile.embassy.gov.au

Canada
Nueva Tajamar 481 Torre Norte, 12th floor. Tel: 2-362-9660.
http://geo.international.gc.ca/latin-america/chile

Ireland
Isidora Goyenechea 3162, 8th floor, Oficina 801, Las Condes.
Tel: 2-245-6616.

New Zealand
Av Isidora Goyenechea 3516.
Tel: 2-231-4204.
www.nzembassy.com/home.cfm?c=16

South African Embassy
Av 11 de Septiembre 2353, 17th floor, Providencia. Tel: 2-231-2862.
www.embajada-sudafrica.cl

UK
Av El Bosque Norte 0125, 3rd floor.
Tel: 2-231-3737. www.britemb.cl

USA
Av Andrés Bello 2800. Tel: 2-232-2600.
www.usembassy.cl

Insurance

Make sure that you are adequately covered for medical expenses or repatriation in the case of accident or illness. A policy should include third party liability, legal assistance, loss of personal possessions (which includes cash, personal documents and traveller's cheques) and should have some provision for cancellations of travel arrangements. Policies that cover stolen handbags or cameras are even better.

Some policies may have clauses saying that they do not cover extreme sport activities such as rafting or paragliding, so be sure to ask beforehand if you intend to partake in such sports. Travel insurance policies can be purchased through the AA, branches of Thomas Cook and most travel agents, as well as online.

Police

Chileans are proud that their police force lacks the corruption that plagues many other Latin American countries. The country is well policed and is relatively safe in most areas. Most police officers are friendly but only rarely will they speak English. Possession of drugs is not tolerated here, and punishments are severe. If you find yourself in serious trouble with the law, contact your embassy.

Directory

Accommodation price guide

A scale of 1–4 stars has been used as a price guide, with 1 star indicating the cheapest option and 4 stars the most expensive. Price bands are based on the average cost of a double room with two people sharing.

★	Up to P10,000
★★	P10,000–P30,000
★★★	P30,000–P60,000
★★★★	Over P60,000
Rates are for high season	

Breakfast will probably be included in the top three bands, but not in the bottom one. Often an additional bed can be added to a room for a fraction of the total. Before you book, be sure to find out whether credit cards are accepted if you are short on cash.

Eating out price guide

The star system below is based on a scale of 1–3 stars, with 1 star indicating the cheapest option and 3 stars indicating the most expensive.

★	Up to P3,000
★★	P3,000–P7,000
★★★	Over P7,000

Addresses are written with the street name first and then the number. When you see the denotation 's/n,' this signifies 'sin numero,' or without number.

You will also find differing presentations of telephone numbers, but each lists the area code first. Area codes vary between these three styles:

x-xxx-xxxx e.g. 2-731-8419

xx-xxx-xxx e.g. 55-851-999

xx-xxx-xxxx e.g. 73-197-5539

SANTIAGO

ACCOMMODATION

Bellavista Hostel ★

Popular and colourful backpacker hostel in the middle of Bellavista's bar and restaurant scene.
Dardignac 184, Bellavista.
Tel: 2-732-8737.
www.bellavistahostel.com.
Metro: Baquedano.

Happy House Hostel ★

Luxury hostel set in a beautifully restored 20th-century mansion. Rooms range from dorms to doubles with private bathrooms.
Catedral 2207, Barrio Brasil.
Tel: 2-688-4849.
www.happyhousehostel.cl.
Metro: Cumming.

Hostal Río Amazonas ★

One of the best value budget accommodation in the city, frequented by a young international crowd.
Av Vicuña Mackenna 47, Lastarria.
Tel: 2-671-9013.
www. hostalrioamazonas.cl.
Metro: Baquedano.

Hotel Foresta ★★
Basic yet cosy, cheery rooms with great amenities for the price.
Subercaseaux 353, Lastarria.
Tel: 2-639-6291.
Metro: Bellas Artes.

Hotel Principado ★★
Great location and comfortable, modern rooms.
Av Vicuña Mackenna 30, Lastarria.
Tel: 2-222-8142.
Metro: Baquedano.

Sheraton ★★★
Very large and well kitted out hotel and event complex across the Río Mapocho.
Av Santa Maria 1742, Providencia.
Tel: 2-233-5000.
www.sheraton.com

Hotel Neruda ★★★★
Luxury hotel in the heart of Providencia, yet lacks the character of its namesake.
Av Pedro De Valdivia 164, Providencia.
Tel: 2-679-0700.
www.hotelneruda.cl.
Metro: Pedro de Valdivia.

Hyatt Regency ★★★★
One of the best hotels in the city, with beautiful mountain views, excellent service and world-class restaurants. Recently completed a $6 million makeover.
Av Kennedy 4061, Las Condes.
Tel: 2-950-1234.
www.hyatt.com

Novotel ★★★★
Modern, comfortable rooms that can often be found online for well below the asking price.
Av Américo Vespucio Norte 1630, Vitacura.
Tel: 2-499-2200.
www.novotel.com

Plaza San Francisco ★★★★
One of the older 5-star hotels in the city, but well maintained. It's just beside San Francisco church. Well equipped to handle any type of traveller or event.
Alameda 816, Centro.
Tel: 2-639-3832.
www.plazasanfrancisco.cl.
Metro: Universidad de Chile.

Ritz Carlton ★★★★
The first Ritz Carlton in South America, this is the best hotel in the city, with the finest amenities and services.
El Alcalde 15, Las Condes.
Tel: 2-470-8500.
www.ritzcarlton.com.
Metro: El Golf.

San Cristobal Tower ★★★★
De luxe pampering and excellent service.
Josefina Edwards de Ferrari 100, Providencia.
Tel: 2-707-1000.
www.starwoodhotels.com.
Metro: Pedro de Valdivia.

EATING OUT

Hansel y Gretel ★
A German tea salon with a country atmosphere in Arrayán.
Los Refugios and El Remanso, El Arrayán.
Tel: 2-321-6073.

El Naturista ★
The best vegetarian place in the city.
Moneda 846, Centro.
Tel: 2-390-5940.
Metro: Universidad de Chile.

Venezia ★
Legendary dive bar with Chilean staples.
Pío Nono 200, Bellavista.
Tel: 2-777-4845.
Metro: Baquedano.

034 ★★
Funky, tiny café with fresh takes on American classics such as carrot cake, waffles and green-tea lemonade.

*Orrego Luco 034,
Providencia.*
Tel: 2-335-0692.
Metro: Pedro de Valdivia.

Blackburn Café ★★

Chic bistro that hosts occasional cooking classes and offers delicious and beautiful-looking dishes for lunching ladies.
Av Alonso de Córdova 4330, Vitacura.
Tel: 2-208-9113.

Cocoa ★★

Peruvian restaurant with great Pisco cocktails and *ceviche* (raw fish marinated in lime), inside an old train.
Lastarria 297, Bellavista.
Tel: 2-632-1272.
Metro: Baquedano.

Etniko ★★

Very trendy sushi bar.
Constitución 172, Bellavista.
Tel: 2-732-0119.
Metro: Baquedano.

Giulia ★★

Northern Italian dishes in a small dining room furnished with olive-green semicircular booths.
Avenida Vitacura 3879, Vitacura.
Tel: 2-228-0023.
Metro Tobalaba.

Mercado Central ★★

Numerous restaurants offering nearly every type of seafood found in the country.
Mercado Central 105, Centro.
Tel: 2-672-3636. Metro: Puente Cal y Canto.

El Mesón Nerudiano ★★

A menu displaying poet Pablo Neruda's favourite dishes.
Dominíca 35, Bellavista.
Tel: 2-737-1542.
Metro: Baquedano.

El Otro Sitio ★★

Laid-back restaurant with Peruvian specialities.
Lopez de Bello 53, Bellavista.
Tel: 2-777-3059.
Metro: Baquedano.

Patagonia ★★

Chocolate and pastry shop run by an Argentine couple.
José Victorino Lastarria 96, Centro.
Tel: 2-664-3830.
Metro: Bellas Artes.

R ★★

Peruvian fusion dishes.
Lastarria 307, Lastarria.
Tel: 2-664-9844.
Metro: Bellas Artes.

Sicosis ★★

Lively café and bar.

José Miguel de la Barra 544, Centro.
Tel: 2-632-4462.
Metro: Bellas Artes.

Amorio ★★★

Chic, glass-fronted building in Bellavista, filled with the young and beautiful. International fusion dishes and an excellent lunch menu makes this one of the best fine dining locations in the city.
Constitución 183, Bellavista.
Tel: 2-777-1454.
Metro: Baquedano.

Astrid y Gaston ★★★

Beautiful satellite restaurant of the original in Lima, Peru, which serves South American recipes with a contemporary touch.
Antonio Bellet 201, Providencia.
Tel: 2-650-9125.
Metro: Manuel Montt.

Confitería Torres ★★★

Restored central landmark serving seafood specialities in front of lively entertainment.
Alameda 1570, Centro.
Tel: 2-688-0751.
Metro: Los Héroes.

Infante 51 ★★★

Basque chef Xabier Zabala prepares perfectly grilled calamari, squid-ink black risotto and seafood-stuffed aubergine.
Av José Miguel Infante 51, Providencia.
Tel: 2-264-3357.
Metro: Salvador.

Restobar KY ★★★

Photographer/chef Juan Pablo Izquierdo's Southeast Asian-inspired menu in a restaurant that's decorated with flea market-esque antiques located in an old rambling house. It's visited by Santiago's yuppie élite and international celebrities.
Av Perú 631, Bellavista.
Tel: 2-777-7245.
Metro: Baquedano.

Santabrasa ★★★

A very stylish, yet classic, Argentine *parrillada* (mixed grill) with a nice wine list.
Av Alonso de Córdova 4260, Vitacura.
Tel: 2-206-4110.

Zully ★★★

French-Asian-Chilean fusion served in a four-storey mansion that was once home to Chilean poet Vicente Huidobro.

Concha y Toro 34, Concha y Toro. Tel: 2-696-3990.
Metro: Los Héroes.

ENTERTAINMENT

Bar Dos Gardenias

Live Latin folk and classical music plus tango several nights a week.
Bello 199, Bellavista.
Tel: 2-474-4534.

Bar Liguria

Hot spot drawing a diverse crowd, offering reasonably priced drinks and a good wine list.
Av Providencia 1373, Providencia.
Tel: 2-253-7914.

Blondie

European-style dance club playing indie and Brit pop, techno and 80s. Frequented mainly by a student crowd.
Alameda 2879, Barrio Brasil.
Tel: 2-681-7793.

Boomerang

Chic bar with loud music and expensive cocktails, popular with foreigners.
Holley 2285, Providencia.
Tel: 2-334-5081.

Etniko

One of the 'it' spots in the city with a multitude of beautiful people at the bar on most nights.

Constitución 172, Bellavista.
Tel: 2-732-0119.
Metro: Baquedano

Habana Salsa

One of the best locations for salsa dancing.
Bucarest 95, Bellavista.
Tel: 2-737-1737.

N'Autin

Mapuche word for 'free', this one time leftist hangout has live indie music on Friday nights.
Av Ricardo Cumming 453, Barrio Brasil.
Tel: 2-671-8410.

Phone Box Pub

British-style pub entered through a big, red phone box.
Av Providencia 1670, Providencia.
Tel: 2-235-9972. Metro: Pedro de Valdivia.

Teatro La Comedia

Edgy comedies and plays for an adult crowd.
Merced 349, Centro.
Tel: 2-639-1523. Metro: Baquedano.

Teatro Municipal

Classic venue for plays, opera, tango and classical music.
Agustinas 794, Centro.
Tel: 2-463-8888.
Metro: Santa Lucía.

Teatro Oriente

Performance art and the occasional classical concert.

Av Valdivia Norte 99, Providencia.
Tel: 2-335-0023.
Metro: Pedro de Valdivia.

Teatro Universidad de Chile

Classical concerts, orchestras and ballets.

Providencia 43, Centro.
Tel: 2-634-5295.
Metro: Baquedano.

Thelonius

The best jazz club in the city, with a range of styles.

Bombero Nuñez 336, Bellavista.
Tel: 2-735-7962.
Metro: Baquedano.

Sport and Leisure

Club de Golf Los Leones (Santiago)

Av Presidente Riesco 3700, Las Condes.
Tel: 2-462-3000.

Club Hípico de Santiago

Beautiful location under the Andes. Once a favourite with the country's élite, it has become dilapidated in recent years. Horse races are held every Friday and alternating Mondays and Wednesdays.

Av Blanca Encalada 2540.
Tel: 2-693-9600.
Metro: Unión Latinoamericana.

Estadio Nacional

Chile's largest football stadium.

Av Grecia 2001.
Tel: 2-238-8102.

Go Fitness & Spa

Av Kennedy 6630, Centro.
Tel: 2-202 4646.

Hipódromo Chile

Horse-racing on Saturdays and most Thursdays.

Av Hipódromo, Independencia.
Tel: 2-270-9237.
Metro: Einstein.

Medialuna de Rancagua

Chile's main rodeo court.

Av España s/n (82km/51 miles south of Santiago).

Powerhouse Gym

Ecomenderos 192, Las Condes.
Tel: 2-366-9911.

Prince of Wales Country Club (Santiago)

Rugby, hockey and golf.

Las Aranas 1901, La Reina.
Tel: 2-277-2025. Metro: Principe de Gales.

VALPARAÍSO

Accommodation

Hostal Luna Sonrisa ★

Restored old house in a great location on the top of Cerro Alegre with beautiful views of the city and coast.

Templeman 833.
Tel: 32-734-117.
www.lunasonrisa.cl

Brighton B&B ★★★

The six rooms in this restored Victorian house are exceptional and have magical views of the city.

Pasaje Atkinson, Cerro Concepción.
Tel: 32-222-3513.
www.brighton.cl

Eating Out

El Cinzano ★

Famous location with hearty food and a lively bar. Open since 1896.

Aníbal Pinto 1182.
Tel: 32-213-043.

Café Columbina ★★

Pricey food in a beautiful setting overlooking the bay.

Pasaje Apolo 91.
Tel: 32-236-254.

Coco Loco ★★

Upscale seafood set in a revolving glass-enclosed dining room.

Blanco 1781.
Tel: 32-227-614.

Pasta y Vino ★★

Trendy new Chilean–Italian fusion restaurant.

Templeman 352.
Tel: 32-496-187.

SPORT AND LEISURE
Club de Golf Marbella (Valparaíso)
Exclusive 18-hole course favoured by politicians.
Av Club de Golf, Cachagua.
Tel: 2-855-8492.

VIÑA DEL MAR
ACCOMMODATION
Girasoles de Agua Santa Guesthouse ★★
Restored Victorian home located on a main street with beautiful views and clean rooms.
Pasaje Monterrey 78.
Tel: 32-248-2339.
Hotel del Mar ★★★★
Luxurious 60-room hotel whose standards far exceed even the best on the central coast.
Av San Martín 199.
Tel: 32-500-800.
www.hoteldelmar.cl

EATING OUT
Divino Pecado ★★
Serves Italian and seafood in an elegant atmosphere.
Av San Martín 180.
Tel: 32-975-790.

ARICA
ACCOMMODATION
Hotel Mar Azul ★
One of the best value deals in the country. This small, cheap hotel is located in the heart of the city and has a small pool, a collection of tropical birds, restaurant and cosy modern rooms with cable TV.
Colón 665.
Tel: 58-256-272.
www.hotelmarazul.cl
Hotel Arica ★★★
Full scale resort located on the waterfront a short walk from the centre of town. Some rooms overlook the rocky shore.
Av San Martín 599.
Tel: 58-254-450. www.
panamericanahoteles.cl

EATING OUT
Maracuyá ★★
Offers excellent seafood as well as beautiful ocean views.
Av San Martín 321.
Tel: 58-227-600.

IQUIQUE
ACCOMMODATION
Hotel Terrado Suites ★★★
Luxury hotel on Playa Cavancha. Prices drop significantly in the low season.
Los Rieles 126.
Tel: 57-437-878.
www.terrado.viajero.cl

BAHÍA INGLESA
EATING OUT
El Plateo ★★
Serves excellent Peruvian and seafood dishes.
On the Malécon s/n.
Tel: 9-826-0007.

SAN PEDRO DE ATACAMA
ACCOMMODATION
Katarpe ★★
Laid-back hotel made of local materials such as stone and *adobe* (mud) with modern amenities including internet connection and a coffee bar. Also runs its own tourist agency.
Atienza 441.
Tel: 55-851-946.
www.katarpe.com
Explora's Hotel de Larache ★★★★
Beautifully designed lodge and spa with stunning desert and mountain views.
Ayllú de Larache, 1km (2/3 mile) from the centre.
Tel: 55-851-110.
www.explora.com

EATING OUT

Adobe ★

Popular place serving
Chilean and
international cuisine.
Also offers good set
meals.
Caracoles 211.
Tel: 55-851-132.

Cuna Restaurant ★★

Atacameño recipes with
a modern flair.
Tocopilla 359.
Tel: 55-851-999.

TALCA

ACCOMMODATION

Casa Donoso ★★★

Beautiful guesthouse
in the vineyard that
can arrange horse tours
and picnics.
Fundo La Oriental,
Camino Palmira Km3.5.
Tel: 71-242-506.
www.casadonoso.com

Viña Tabontinaja ★★★★

Chic agrotourism resort,
which arranges tastings
and wine therapies.
Camino Constitución Km
20, San Javier.
Tel: 73-197-5539.
www.gillmore.cl.

SAN FERNANDO

ACCOMMODATION

Viña Casa Silva ★★★

Seven-room wine resort
on a small vineyard in
the Colchagua Valley.
Camino El Tambo, San
Fernando.
Tel: 72-913-091.
www.casasilva.cl

PUCÓN

ACCOMMODATION

¡école! ★★

Very popular hotel with
international
backpackers. Arranges
many new age and
adventure activities.
Rooms fill up weeks in
advance during summer.
General Urrutia 592.
Tel: 45-441-675.
www.ecole.cl

Del Volcán Apart
Hotel ★★★

Family-oriented hotel
with large rooms with
kitchenettes. Ideal for
four–six people. Rates
drop dramatically in low
season.
Fresia 430.
Tel: 2-594-0424. www.
aparthotel.pucon.com

Gran Hotel Pucón ★★★★

Set on the shore of Lago
Villarica, this is the best
hotel in town. It's large,
has good restaurants,
great views, reasonable
prices, and offers travel
services.
Clemente Holzapfel 190.
Tel: 42-913-300.
www.granhotelpucon.cl

EATING OUT

La Marmita de
Pericles ★★

Offers fondue, raclette,
pasta and a number of
Swiss dishes.
Fresia 300.
Tel: 45-441-114.

Viva Perú ★★

Traditional Peruvian
dishes served in an
elegant atmosphere.
Lincoyán 372.
Tel: 45-444-025.

ENTERTAINMENT

El Bosque

Chic spot for older,
upscale and refined
tourists.
Av O'Higgins 524.
Tel: 45-443-226.

Mamas & Tapas

DJs spin music under
video screens that play
adventure sports images,
in one of the most
popular clubs in town.
Av O'Higgins 587.
Tel: 45-449-002.

VALDIVIA

ACCOMMODATION

Hotel Naguilán ★★★

Attractive riverfront

hotel in a restored 19th-century shipbuilding company. Rooms in the new wing tend to be much better. The hotel has its own dock from which it arranges boat excursions.
General Lagos 1927.
Tel: 63-212-851.
www.hotelnaguilan.com

EATING OUT
Cervceceria Kuntsmann ★★
Hearty German specialities paired with the finest beers in the country, which are brewed on site.
On Isla Teja, 3km (2 miles) northwest of the centre.
Tel: 63-292-969.

ENTERTAINMENT
Arte-Bar
Live bossa and rock music plus literary readings.
San Carlos 169.
Tel: 63-256-968.
Ocio Restobar
Sleek lounge with occasional live music and DJs. Would be hip in Paris, let alone Valdivia.
Arauco 102.
Tel: 63-345-090.

FRUTTILAR
ACCOMMODATION
Termas de Puyehue ★★★
Beautiful hotel and thermal spa set amid lush temperate forests on the shores of Lago Puyuhue.
Ruta 215 Km 76.
Tel: 02-293-6000.
www.puyehue.cl

PUERTO MONTT
ACCOMMODATION
Hotel Viento Sur ★★★
Restored colonial house with great sea views.
Ejército 200.
Tel: 65-258-701.
www.hotelvientosur.cl

EATING OUT
Chilotito Marino ★
Chilote seafood including *curanto* (meat, potato and shellfish stew).
Angelmó Palafitos.
Tel: 65-277-585.
Fogón de Cotelé ★★★
Brazilian-style steakhouse. Order your meat or fish by weight.
Balneario Pelluco.
Tel: 65-278-000.

CASTRO
EATING OUT
Años Luz ★★
Contemporary restaurant serving an array of mouth-watering international and Chilote dishes.
San Martín 309.
Tel: 65-532-700.
Sacho ★★
The best seafood in Castro and a good place to eat *curanto* (meat, potato and shellfish stew, traditionally cooked in a hole in the ground).
Thompson 213.
Tel: 65-632-079.

ENTERTAINMENT
Pub K-Nos
Trendy and modern club with DJs spinning the latest techno and trance.
Blanco Encalada 350.
Tel: 65-633-110.

ACHAO
EATING OUT
Mar y Velas ★★
Serves up excellent fish and shellfish in a location overlooking the market and harbour.
Serrano 2.
Tel: 65-661-375.

PUYUHUAPI
ACCOMMODATION
Termas de Puyuhuapi ★★★★
Very chic resort and spa set amid lush forest on

an isolated sound and access to numerous thermal pools.
Seno Ventisquero.
Tel: 67-325-103. www. termasdepuyuhuapi.cl

PUNTA ARENAS
ACCOMMODATION
Hostal South Pacific ★
Large, light rooms in a laid-back atmosphere and a friendly host.
Errázuriz 860.
Tel: 09-154-2969.
www.hostalsouthpacific.cl
Hotel Boutique Oro Fueguino ★★
Twelve bright and cheery rooms overlooking the Magellan Strait.
Fagnano 356.
Tel: 61-249-401.
www.orofueguino.com
Hotel José Nogueira ★★★★
Elegant hotel in a restored mansion from the wool baron era.
Bories 959.
Tel: 61-711-000.
www.hotelnogueira.com

EATING OUT
Lomit's ★
Popular diner offering excellent sandwiches and grilled meats.
Menéndez 722.
Tel: 61-243-399.

Santino Bar e Cucina ★
Serves pizza, sandwiches, crêpes and seafood.
Av Colón 657.
Tel: 61-710-882.
Hotel José Nogueira ★★★
The best restaurant in town, with regional and international dishes, as well as *centolla* (king crab).
Bories 959.
Tel: 61-248-840.

ENTERTAINMENT
Olijoe Pub
Beautiful English bar, offering a number of draught beers.
Errázuriz 970.
Tel: 61-223-728.

PUERTO NATALES
ACCOMMODATION
Altiplanico Sur ★★★★
Brilliantly designed hotel with world-class amenities in a quiet spot overlooking Seno de la Última Esperanza.
Huerto Familiar 282.
Tel: 61-412-525.
www.altiplanico.cl
Hotel Indigo Patagonia ★★★★
Recently opened charismatic and chic boutique hotel and spa.
Ladrilleros 105.
Tel: 61-413-609.

EATING OUT
La Oveja Negra ★★
Specialises in lamb and *centolla* (king crab) fondue. Located just off the main square.
Tomas Rogers 169.
Tel: 61-410-772.

TORRES DEL PAINE
ACCOMMODATION
Posada Río Serrano ★★
Basic lodge in a convenient location amid alpine rivers and lakes.
Across from the Administración.
Tel: 61-412-911.
Explora's Hotel Salto Chico ★★★★
One of the world's most stunning nature lodges, with prices to match. Beautiful views of Parque Nacional Torres del Paine and Lago Pehoé.
Lago Pehoé, Parque Nacional Torres del Paine.
Tel: 2-395-2580.
www.explora.com
Hostería Lago Grey ★★★★
First-class amenities and dining in view of Glacier Grey.
Lautaro Navarro 1061.
Tel: 61-225-986. www. turismolagogrey.com

Index

Acknowledgements

Thomas Cook wishes to thank the photographers, picture libraries and other organisations for the loan of the photographs reproduced in this book, to whom copyright in the photographs belongs.

STOCK.XCHNG/alge12 82
FLICKR/grom 131
WIKIMEDIA COMMONS/Reinhard Jahn 51
WORLD PICTURES/PHOTOSHOT 1, 50

All remaining photographs were taken by NICHOLAS GILL.

Proofreading: RICHARD HALL for CAMBRIDGE PUBLISHING MANAGEMENT LTD

Maps: PCGRAPHICS UK LTD

Index: KAROLIN THOMAS for CAMBRIDGE PUBLISHING MANAGEMENT LTD

SEND YOUR THOUGHTS TO
BOOKS@THOMASCOOK.COM

We're committed to providing the very best up-to-date information in our travel guides and constantly strive to make them as useful as they can be. You can help us to improve future editions by letting us have your feedback. If you've made a wonderful discovery on your travels that we don't already feature, if you'd like to inform us about recent changes to anything that we do include, or if you simply want to let us know your thoughts about this guidebook and how we can make it even better – we'd love to hear from you.

Send us ideas, discoveries and recommendations today and then look out for your valuable input in the next edition of this title.

Emails to the above address, or letters to Travellers Project Editor, Thomas Cook Publishing, PO Box 227, Coningsby Road, Peterborough PE3 8SB, UK.

Please don't forget to let us know which title your feedback refers to!